Sustainable Development Goals Series

The **Sustainable Development Goals Series** is Springer Nature's inaugural cross-imprint book series that addresses and supports the United Nations' seventeen Sustainable Development Goals. The series fosters comprehensive research focused on these global targets and endeavours to address some of society's greatest grand challenges. The SDGs are inherently multidisciplinary, and they bring people working across different fields together and working towards a common goal. In this spirit, the Sustainable Development Goals series is the first at Springer Nature to publish books under both the Springer and Palgrave Macmillan imprints, bringing the strengths of our imprints together.

The Sustainable Development Goals Series is organized into eighteen subseries: one subseries based around each of the seventeen respective Sustainable Development Goals, and an eighteenth subseries, "Connecting the Goals", which serves as a home for volumes addressing multiple goals or studying the SDGs as a whole. Each subseries is guided by an expert Subseries Advisor with years or decades of experience studying and addressing core components of their respective Goal.

The SDG Series has a remit as broad as the SDGs themselves, and contributions are welcome from scientists, academics, policymakers, and researchers working in fields related to any of the seventeen goals. If you are interested in contributing a monograph or curated volume to the series, please contact the Publishers: Zachary Romano [Springer; zachary.romano@springer.com] and Rachael Ballard [Palgrave Macmillan; rachael.ballard@palgrave.com].

Chukwuemeka Osuigwe

Economic Development of Rural Areas

Policies and Strategies for Rural Development and Economic Growth

palgrave
macmillan

Chukwuemeka Osuigwe
University of Johannesburg
Gauteng, South Africa

ISSN 2523-3084 ISSN 2523-3092 (electronic)
Sustainable Development Goals Series
ISBN 978-3-032-10571-4 ISBN 978-3-032-10572-1 (eBook)
https://doi.org/10.1007/978-3-032-10572-1

This Palgrave Macmillan imprint is published by the registered company Springer Nature Switzerland AG
The registered company address is: Gewerbestrasse 11, 6330 Cham, Switzerland

This book is dedicated to those who genuinely plan and support sustainable development in Africa. To my lovely wife, Sanelisile Mbali Osuigwe, and our children, Ugochukwu, Amara, and Aku, for the support and patience. It is also dedicated to the family of Osuigwe for their support, my late father, who travelled to many rural communities to teach and pioneer agricultural production, and my mother for her encouragement.

Preface

Over the past decade, many African countries, particularly Nigeria, have faced significant economic challenges. As a result, there is a growing need to develop rural areas and boost their economic potential. The goal is to enhance the quality of life and economic well-being of people living in rural areas by promoting holistic and integrated development approaches, encouraging community participation, and leveraging technology and innovation to achieve this goal. Identifying and harnessing the growth potential in rural areas is a complex process that involves developing the human and physical environments. By doing so, it will attract investment and draw attention to the untapped resources found in rural areas, which can drive economic growth. Cultivating these resources, including indigenous agriculture, tourism, crafts, minerals, talents, skills, biodiversity, and infrastructure, requires a rigorous process involving the active participation of rural communities. A comprehensive rural development plan can lead to a better quality of life and significantly reduce social and economic challenges.

Despite these growth opportunities, rural areas in Africa face numerous limitations and challenges that hinder investment and economic growth. These include inadequate infrastructure, limited access to essential services and social facilities, low population density, and dispersed populations in many parts of Africa, as well as limited economic opportunities and poor governance due to ineffective leadership. Rural areas in Africa are home to a large number of low-income groups and a higher percentage of impoverished individuals. This book highlights the potential, risks, and challenges of rural areas and provides strategic plans that generate innovative ideas for sustainable rural development.

The book offers governments, traditional authorities, private investors, organisations, community leaders, non-governmental agencies, and other development entities, including community workers, the chance to adopt a holistic approach to rural development. It serves as a framework of reference for development programmes in rural areas, providing valuable guidance to governments and policymakers, as well as strategies for problem-solving efforts aimed at enhancing the quality of rural life. The book will establish a database for future studies and act as a vital reference resource for planners, multilateral organisations, non-governmental organisations (NGOs), and others interested in rural development.

Gauteng, South Africa Chukwuemeka Osuigwe

Acknowledgements

I want to express my gratitude to my wife, Mrs. Sanelisile Mbali Osuigwe, for her assistance in editing this book while pursuing her MBA studies and working as a full-time employee. She also identified several opportunities that could foster rural development in Africa, particularly in South Africa. Thank you for your love and encouragement.

I appreciate Professor Felix Okonta for his professional guidance in bringing this book to fruition. My thanks also go to Professor Thulisile Mphambukeli for the support in publishing the book.

The Idea That Birthed This Book

Over the past decade, from 2015 to 2025, I have seen many friends, relatives, and acquaintances lose their jobs in Nigeria, South Africa, and other parts of Africa. Unfortunately, I have also witnessed numerous companies shutting down, particularly in Nigeria, where the cost of doing business has soared, making importation the most affordable option. These problems arise from inadequate leadership and inconsistencies in governance and policy implementation in Nigeria. This has impacted companies' ability to operate efficiently. For instance, on January 1, 2024, the Corporate Affairs Commission (CAC, 2024), a government agency of Nigeria responsible for the formation and management of companies in Nigeria, published a public notice detailing 9,114 companies set to be struck off their register. Of these, 24 were large companies that closed between 2020 and 2024. The notable large companies that have closed since 2020 are as follows.

Furthermore, the Nigeria Deposit Insurance Corporation (NDIC) listed the following banks that have closed since 2006.

Having seen firsthand how small businesses struggle to survive in the face of high inflation, I have witnessed the devastating impact on their resources and their ability to stay afloat. The closure of these companies has led to the loss of thousands of jobs, affecting families and pushing many into poverty. I have seen families resort to begging for food to keep their hopes up for tomorrow. Social and economic challenges have eroded the purchasing power of many individuals, leaving them with little to no disposable income. I have observed young people's hopes for a better future being crushed, as they turn to sports betting due to a lack of employment opportunities or the means to start a business. These struggles and

Year	Companies that Closed
2020	1. Standard Biscuits Nigeria Ltd 2. NASCO Fibre Product Ltd 3. Union Trading Company Nigeria PLC 4. Deli Foods Nigeria Ltd
2021	1. Tower Aluminium Nigeria PLC 2. Framan Industries Ltd 3. Stone Industries Ltd 4. Mufex Nigeria Company Ltd 5. Surest Foam Ltd
2022	1. Universal Rubber Company Ltd 2. Mother's Pride Ventures Ltd 3. Errand Products Nigeria Ltd 4. Gorgeous Metal Makers Ltd
2023	1. Unilever Nigeria PLC 2. Procter & Gamble Nigeria 3. GlaxoSmithKline Consumer Nigeria Ltd 4. Sanofi-Aventis Nigeria Ltd 5. Equinox Nigeria 6. Bolt Food & Jumia Food Nigeria
2024	1. Microsoft Nigeria 2. Total Energies Nigeria (impacted by divestment strategies) 3. Kimberly-Clark Nigeria 4. Diageo PLC

Source CAC (2024)

concerns have driven me to explore options for Africa that could change the narrative for better economic growth, job creation, and entrepreneurial development. The search for a better solution gave birth to this book, **"Development of Rural Areas Potentials and Capacities: Policy and Strategy Direction for Sustainable Rural Development Plan and National Economic Growth".**

Name Of Bank Under Liquidation	Date Of Closure
African Express Bank	16 January 2006
Allstates Trust Bank	16 January 2006
Assurance Bank	16 January 2006
City Express Bank	16 January 2006
Eagle Bank Limited	16 January 2006
Fortune International Bank	16 January 2006
Gulf Bank	16 January 2006
Hallmark Bank	16 January 2006
Lead bank	16 January 2006
Liberty Bank	16 January 2006
Metropolitan Bank	16 January 2006
Trade Bank	16 January 2006
African International Bank	1 August 2013
Bank PHB	5 August 2011
Spring Bank	5 August 2011
Afri Bank	5 August 2011

Source NDIC. https://ndic.gov.ng/failure-resolution/closed-financial-institutions/

Contents

About the Author

Dr. Chukwuemeka Ezenwa Osuigwe is an Associate Senior Researcher at the University of Johannesburg and Director of Sanemy Development Consultants. At the time of writing this book, he had just completed his second term in office, serving as President of the Mbaise Welfare Association in South Africa. Dr. Chukwuemeka Ezenwa Osuigwe is a qualified town and regional planner and researcher. He graduated with Honours in Urban and Regional Planning from Abia State University in 1996. He earned a master's degree in urban and Regional Planning from the University of KwaZulu-Natal in 2005. In 2023, he completed his Ph.D. in Urban and Regional Planning, specialising in Special Economic Zones, at the University of Johannesburg. Dr. Chukwuemeka Osuigwe is professionally registered with the South African Council for Planners (SACPLAN) and is a member of the South African Planning Institute (SAPI). He has authored two book publications.

1. Leadership and Economic Development Challenges in Post-Colonial Africa: Creating Inclusive Economic Growth by Palgrave Macmillan and Springer
2. Shopping Leakage by VDM Verlag Dr. Müller

Dr. Chukwuemeka Osuigwe has published the following article and book chapter.

1. Article: Special Economic Zones (SEZs) Establishments: Lessons from International Experiences for South Africa, published by International Conference on Industrial Engineering and Operations Management (IEOM)
2. Co-authored a chapter on this book, "Contemporary South Africa and the Political Economy of Regional Development": Titled, "Implications of the African Continental Free Trade Area (AFCFTA) and South Africa's Special Economic Zone Policies for the Integration of the Southern African Development Community".

He boasts a wealth of experience in policy and strategy development. With over 25 years of experience, he has practised as a town planner, strategist, local economic developer, and researcher. Throughout his career, he has made significant contributions to the development of numerous townships in South Africa, developed policies, assessed various projects, and managed projects from start to finish.

Acronyms and Abbreviations

ADB	African Development Bank
AFCFTA	African Continental Free Trade Area
AU	African Union
CAADP	Comprehensive Africa Agriculture Development Programme
CAC	Corporate Affairs Commission
CRDP	Comprehensive Rural Development Programme
DDM	District Development Model
DFFE	Department of Forestry, Fishing, and Environment
DFRRI	Directorate for Food, Roads, and Rural Infrastructure
DRDLR	Department of Rural Development and Land Reforms
EU	European Union
FS	Free State
GDP	Gross Domestic Product
GEEP	Enterprise and Empowerment Programme
GIS	Geographical Information System
ICA	Infrastructure Consortium for Africa
IDP	Integrated Development Plan
IFAD	International Fund for Agricultural Development
IFI	International Financial Institutions
ILO	International Labour Organisation
IRP	Integrated Rural Development
KPI	Key Performance Indicators
MAMSER	Mass Mobilisation for Social Justice and Economic Recovery
MDG	Millennium Development Goal

NAPEP	National Poverty Eradication Programme
NARYSEC	National Rural Youth Service Corps
NDE	National Directorate for Employment
NDIC	Nigeria Deposit Insurance Corporation
NDP	National Development Plan
NEED	National Economic Empowerment and Development
NEPA	National Electrical Power Authority
NEPAD	New Partnership for Africa Development
NGO	Non-Governmental Organisation
NNDP	Nigeria National Development Plan.
NSIP	National Social Investment Programme
OECD	Organisation for Economic Co-operation and Development
PPP	Public and Private Participation
R&G	Research and Development
RBDA	River Basin Development Authority
SARD	Sustainable Agricultural and Rural Development
SDG	Sustainable Development Goal
SMME	Small, Medium, and Micro Enterprises
SWOT	Strength, Weakness, Opportunity, and Threat.
TREP	Township and Rural Entrepreneurship Programme
UNDP	United Nations Development Programme

List of Figures

List of Tables

1 Introduction

Creating comprehensive rural development plans in African countries is crucial for achieving sustainable national economic growth and development, fostering social unity and inclusion, and ensuring environmental sustainability. This will boost technology and innovation, adding value to Africa's development, economic progress, and integration. According to Houngbo (2014), increasing agricultural output and building a robust rural economy are essential for Africa. If done correctly, this approach would create millions of jobs, generate wealth, promote inclusion, ensure food security, strengthen resilience to crises, and foster social and political harmony. Rural development would help bridge the significant gap in infrastructure and economic progress between rural and urban areas in Africa. The quality of life, human development, opportunities, educational standards, access to healthcare, infrastructure, and social conditions in rural areas typically fall behind those in urban areas. Despite these challenges, rural development planning often focuses on agricultural production rather than adopting a comprehensive approach to social and economic development.

There are various definitions of rural development, reflecting the complex and multifaceted nature of rural areas. Mosher (1978) describes a progressive rural area as having several key elements, including a market, access to roads, advanced farming methods, and new technologies for development. According to Lassey (1977, p. 2), rural development is "the process of identifying the complex factors contributing to the creation and change of a social and/or physical entity; studying the interrelationship and interactions of those factors in terms of their relative or specific influences; determining as precisely as possible the degree to which specific units of change in any factor contribute to a change in one or more other factors; predicting how changes in one factor ought to be made so

C. Osuigwe, *Economic Development of Rural Areas*, Sustainable Development Goals Series, https://doi.org/10.1007/978-3-032-10572-1_1

that future society will achieve an improvement in human welfare without damaging the environment on which larger generations depend; and finally, acting on predictions to achieve a more satisfactory human and physical environment". Proponents of industrialisation highlight the industrial potential of rural development, while advocates of "back-to-the-land" see modernised agriculture with efficient use of natural resources like land, fisheries, forestry, livestock, and minerals, as well as allied processing operations, as holding the promise of faster economic development. This book synthesises various schools of thought and definitions to develop a comprehensive approach to rural development within a progressive socio-political context, ultimately fostering dynamic economic prosperity in rural areas.

According to Keke (1998), local resources can be tapped into to create affordable and development-inducing business projects. However, without a thorough understanding of rural social and economic potentials, it is impossible to achieve sustainable and dynamic rural development, which in turn is essential for national economic growth and modernisation. This necessitates the growth and development of both rural and urban sectors. The book highlights the challenges facing sustainable rural development, including a lack of skills, inadequate infrastructure, limited access to social amenities such as education and healthcare, financial exclusion, poor governance, land ownership issues, and environmental degradation. It also examines the roles of governmental structures and their implications for rural development. Furthermore, international and African case studies are analysed to draw on experiences and compare approaches to rural development planning in different regions, including transitional, developed countries, developing countries, and African countries like Nigeria and South Africa.

This book aims to enhance rural development plans and strategies in Africa, to improve the economic and social conditions of rural communities, attracting investment, and promoting a sustainable environment. Using a qualitative approach, the book draws on interviews, spatial data from selected rural areas, observations, archival documents, online data, and analyses of government systems. It presents its findings through reports, charts, graphs, tables, and figures. The book offers strategic and policy recommendations, as well as options for developing smart rural areas. In Africa, a substantial proportion of the population lives in rural areas, making it crucial for national development to incorporate holistic and sustainable rural development strategies.

1.1 The Problem

According to the World Bank, Africa's rural population is estimated to be 718,293,979 in 2023, accounting for nearly half of the continent's total population. However, this growth is occurring without sufficient social and economic planning to bring these communities into Africa's social and economic hubs. The resulting surge has led to high unemployment rates, income inequality, and limited social and economic policies that often neglect the needs of the most vulnerable rural communities. Over the past decade, Sub-Saharan Africa has seen extreme poverty, especially in rural areas, partly due to inadequate access to clean water, sanitation, healthcare, and other basic living standards. Moreover, rural populations face significant obstacles to education, healthcare, and low income. These conditions have contributed to preventable diseases and deaths.

Challenges in rural Africa are complex and multifaceted, marked by stagnation and underdevelopment despite the continent's vast natural resources (Osuigwe, 2024). These issues stem primarily from inadequate government interventions, poor policy-making, and ineffective strategic planning. Moreover, even when plans and budgets are set for rural development, corruption undermines their impact, diverting funds meant for rural advancement into private hands. This has hindered substantial progress in rural development across the African continent.

Addressing rural development in Africa is a complex and multifaceted issue. It stems from letdowns in leadership at both the community and national levels, with the primary issue being at the national level. As a Chinese proverb aptly states, "fish rots from the head". In Africa, dictatorship and poor governance have long posed persistent problems that severely hinder rural development. The continent faces more conflicts than any other region, significantly impacting rural development and economic growth. In Nigeria's Middle Belt (which comprises Adamawa, Benue, Kaduna, Plateau, Nasarawa, and Taraba), many rural farmers have been displaced by herdsmen who roam with cattle and guns. In some instances, this has led to the deaths of hundreds of farmers, creating further poverty and destitution. According to John (2020), estimates for 2019 indicate that at least 160,000 displaced individuals are scattered across Benue State, with the majority being rural farmers. However, official estimates do not yet account for the many thousands more displaced in 2020. Furthermore, over 58,400 Cameroonian refugees reside in Nigeria, predominantly in Middle Belt states, with more than 8000 in Benue. The problem extends beyond conflict, encompassing numerous other issues, as outlined below, which appear remarkably intractable. The significant problems observed in African rural areas and data from secondary sources, such as books and articles, are:

1. The problem of revenue generation.
2. Poverty
3. Infrastructural development.
4. Lack of skills.
5. Unemployment.
6. Industrialisation.
7. Commercialisation.
8. Tourism.
9. Problem of tapping or exploiting local resources.
10. Problem of low agricultural production.
11. Innovation.

Among the challenges mentioned earlier, poverty in rural areas is the most pressing and significant issue, primarily driven by other factors. The poverty rate in Africa is alarmingly high, affecting daily life. According to Alkire et al. (2021, p. 2), "In sub-Saharan Africa, 556 million people live in multidimensional poverty; 82% of them reside in rural areas. Severe poverty remains a major challenge for many countries in sub-Saharan Africa; in 19 of the 36 countries, more than half of the population, as measured by the Multidimensional Poverty Index (MPI), are living in severe poverty. Nearly a third (31%) of sub-Saharan Africa's population is in severe multidimensional poverty". The extent of poverty in sub-Saharan Africa is illustrated in the figure below, which compares its poverty levels to those of other regions worldwide.

Fig 1.1 illustrates that extreme poverty is not confined to Sub-Saharan Africa. The World Bank (2024) states that in 2000, a quarter of the extremely poor population lived in Sub-Saharan Africa or fragile states. By 2014, this proportion had increased, with every second person in extreme poverty residing in Sub-Saharan Africa. The report emphasises a notable rise in the number of extremely poor individuals in fragile and conflict-affected situations within Sub-Saharan Africa in the late 2010s, as countries with large, impoverished populations became fragile, such as Niger and Nigeria. By 2024, three-quarters of the extremely poor were in Sub-Saharan Africa or fragile and conflict-affected areas, with 42 percent of the global extreme poor living in fragile and conflict-affected situations in Sub-Saharan Africa (World Bank, 2024). To address poverty, comprehensive rural development strategies are vital.

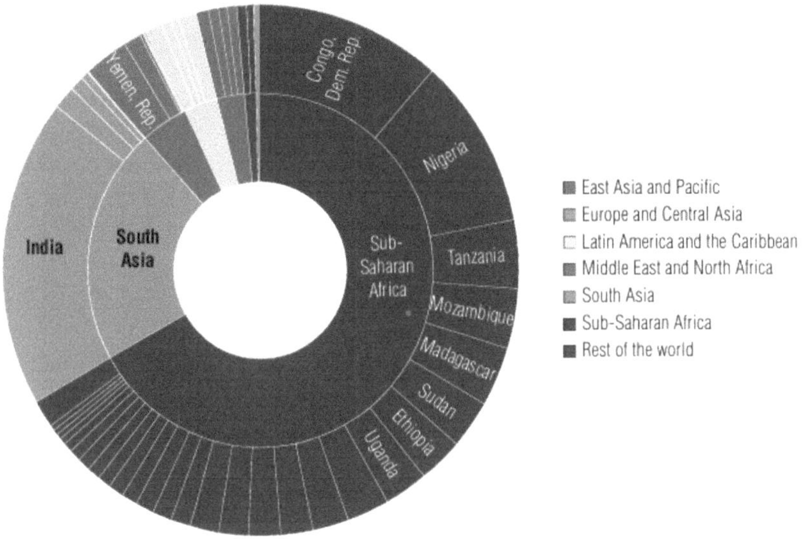

Fig. 1.1 Extreme poverty ($2.15 per person per day) is concentrated in Sub-Saharan Africa.Source World Bank (2024)

Despite the issues and challenges, the paramount question is: if all the resources are available, what would the local governments do?

1. Develop rural areas and their economy.
2. Increase income.
3. Stimulate employment.
4. Increase revenue generation.

One of the key factors in rural development could be the above. However, local governments rely mainly on "self-generated funds" from revenue collection. To increase revenue, they employ more aggressive collection techniques, which are unsustainable and place an additional financial strain on rural residents. Many rural areas are struggling with poverty, poor infrastructure, limited access to technology, high unemployment, inadequate social services, and substandard living conditions, making rent increases and revenue collection unjustifiable. Moreover, the lack of jobs and low incomes in rural areas add to the burden of local government taxes and rates. National government revenue allocations are another source of income for local governments that champion rural development; however, corruption within the political leadership makes achieving rural development unsustainable.

It is undeniable that there are no rural development projects; however, these projects are often driven by politics and are unsustainable. Many rural communities barely felt the impact of these development projects. Because they were politically motivated, which were not anchored on community livelihoods and indigenous knowledge development and improvement, this can be attributed to several factors, including a lack of transparency and accountability in project execution, as well as insufficient community involvement and management. As a result, the absence of inclusivity impacts the sustainability of these projects. Many of these initiatives are poorly located due to political interference, rendering them inaccessible to rural residents.

Furthermore, there are virtually no industrial establishments, and in many cases, no industrial development, in rural areas to cater to the employment needs of rural people. This has led to a few hands being employed, resulting in out-migration. The following questions are crucial in alleviating the critical nature of the problems in rural areas of Africa.

1. What can be done to attract industries to the rural areas?
2. What type of industries could be attracted?
3. What kind of commercial activities and market systems are needed
4. What should be done to mechanise agriculture
5. What role will tourism play in developing rural areas
6. What is the role of mining in rural areas
7. What type of communication, IT systems, and greener energy could lead to smart rural and community development
8. What indigenous knowledge could be improved to add value to rural development

From the above, it is therefore essential to develop aims and objectives that this book aims to achieve.

1.2 Aims and Objectives

1. Identify rural challenges.
2. Identify the state of rural infrastructure in Africa.
3. Identify policies and strategies that affect rural development.
4. To discover and identify rural resources and potentials.
5. Provide case studies on rural development plans
6. Examine the structure and role of governments in rural development plans
7. Recommend the development of rural integrated development planning through a holistic strategic development framework that supports smart rural communities.

The challenges identified in rural areas of Africa and Nigeria align with the aims and objectives of this book, as listed above. The book also aims to address the challenges faced by rural areas that impede rural development to enhance social and economic opportunities. The achievement of the aims and objectives will lead to the creation of opportunities, empowering rural communities, generating employment, reducing migration from rural areas to urban areas, or encouraging migration from urban areas to rural areas. The primary aim and objective are to focus on creating sustainable rural economic growth that is appealing to the rural settlements.

2 Conceptual Framework and Theoretical Framework

Abstract

This chapter explores the multifaceted field of rural development, focusing on the social, economic, political, and environmental dimensions that aim to improve the living standards and economic opportunities of rural populations, particularly in Africa. It delves into the conceptual foundations of rural development, examining various forms of rural settlements and the factors influencing them. The document defines development as a process that enhances individuals' capabilities, resources, and conversion factors, emphasising the importance of holistic and inclusive approaches. It highlights the challenges and potential of Africa's rural economy, noting the significant role of agriculture and small-scale mining. The differences between economic growth and economic development are discussed, with a focus on qualitative improvements in living standards. The document also emphasises the importance of inclusive rural development planning, sustainable rural development, and the integration of rural and urban economies. Current trends in rural development, such as digital connectivity and the promotion of sustainable agriculture, are explored. Theoretical frameworks, including Integrated Rural Development Theory, Economic Base Theory, and Big Push Theory, are presented to guide rural development planning and interventions.

C. Osuigwe, *Economic Development of Rural Areas*, Sustainable Development Goals Series, https://doi.org/10.1007/978-3-032-10572-1_2

2.1 Introduction

This book's conceptual framework sets out the core concepts of rural development and the economy. In contrast, the theoretical framework provides a broader perspective that informs the conceptual framework and guides the book's interventions. The conceptual framework is a narrative representation that structures the book's ideology and concepts related to the rural development problem and the planned strategic phenomenon. The theoretical framework provides the perspective that guides the conceptual framework and the intervention. It draws upon the concepts and established theories to explain the relationships and processes in rural development and economic growth. Furthermore, many people may be confused about specific words and their meanings until they are clarified. For example, a reader might be confused about the difference between rural settlement and rural development planning. Keywords like "rural" can be confusing, depending on the region of the world. Therefore, their examination helps the reader understand the type of rural area the book explores. The concepts and theories identified are examined and explained below.

2.1.1 Rural Settlement/Area

Rural settlements are generally considered to be outside the urban or township setting. Most rural settlements are influenced by the topography of the area, climate and weather, soil, water sources, type of land tenure, and social patterns. Rural areas can be considered spatial units of production for both the informal sector and a few formal sectors, encompassing commercial activities, mining, and most agricultural activities. Rural settlements are fundamental social spaces formed by residents based on their production and living needs, serving as the basic units of traditional agrarian societies (Yao, 2019). Some researchers have defined rurality in terms of three aspects of land use: the relevance of architecture, landscape, and lifestyle in rural settlements (Marsden & Mooney, 2006; Cloke, 1985).

African rural areas are generally associated with agriculture and, to a lesser extent, rural mining for construction, which still relies on manual and local efforts. The implication is that rural areas depend on the agricultural sector for income, employment, and other livelihood opportunities. Despite its contribution to the national economy and GDP, rural areas in Nigeria remain very poor and deeply neglected (IFAD, 2011), a situation that is also prevalent in most rural areas across Africa. Rural settlements take various forms, which are determined by their geographical location, the types of road networks, and even climatic conditions. The forms of rural settlements are influenced by economic activities, culture, and topography, and these forms are explained below.

1. **Compact and Nucleated Rural Settlements: These are rural settlements characterised by** compact and closely built-up areas. The settlements are concentrated, and several factors could contribute to this, including commercial activities, mining, and light industrial settlements. This settlement is typically found in the eastern part of Nigeria and is mainly inhabited by the Igbo ethnic group. All the villages in Eastern Nigeria are nuclear settlements in spatial form. These rural settlements have evolved into semi-urban areas, acquiring many of the characteristics of a town. Some of these settlements can be found in Kano, Northern Nigeria, and certain parts of Gauteng, South Africa.
2. **Linear Rural Settlements:** Linear rural settlements are characterised by houses built along roads, riverbanks, or coastlines, and most often, agricultural land extending behind the buildings. Most settlement patterns in Eastern Nigeria and KwaZulu in South Africa are linear patterns located along major roads or major road intersections and on the coastline in KwaZulu-Natal. They are also situated along river basins such as the Delta of Nigeria and the Middle Belt of Nigeria. They are found along transport routes and provide easy access to the rural settlement for their social and economic activities. Some are found along the coastline, which serves as both a water source and a transportation route.
3. **Semi-clustered or Fragmented Settlement:** This type of rural settlement is neither closely clustered nor dispersed. However, the settlements might cover more areas than clustered or nuclear rural settlements. This settlement could be situated in rural mining towns, agricultural areas, or hilly regions. These are more common in the Western and Northern Parts of Nigeria. They could also be found in some parts of the Northwest and the Free State of South Africa.
4. **Dispersed or Isolated Settlement:** In this type of settlement, the houses are separated; they are not closely knitted nor semi-closely knitted. Dispersed settlements or isolated settlements in rural areas are characterised by groups of houses separated from each other by physical characteristics or agricultural practices. The type of settlement houses is scattered over a vast area and lacks a specific pattern. They can be found in northern Nigeria. They are predominantly located in the agricultural areas of South Africa, rural areas of KwaZulu-Natal, and the Eastern Cape of South Africa.

One significant observation in the Eastern part of Nigeria and some parts of South Africa is that some clustered and nuclear rural settlements are transforming into towns. The transformation is due to private and public investments in infrastructure, commercial, mining, industrial, agro-business, construction, higher education institutions, electricity, and many other services.

2.1.2 Development

What is development? Arkhangelskaia and Perfilyeva (2023, p. 5) explained development in the following patterns and concepts.

1. "Capability, at its most elementary and individual level, is "the freedom to achieve valuable human functions. Hence, capabilities are opportunities that allow people the autonomy to do or be things and to achieve the quality of life".
2. "Resources are material or measurable metrics such as income".
3. "Conversion factors shape the processes of transforming resources into opportunities and capabilities into functioning and may be differentiated into personal, social and environmental conversion factors.

I. Personal: disability, for example.
II. Social conversion factor: structural constraints, such as policies, social or cultural norms, and legal rules.
III. Environmental conversion factors: physical features of the location or built environment".

Nyerere (1977), the former president of Kenya, described the development as "a process which enables human beings to realise their potential, build self-confidence, and lead lives of dignity and fulfilment. It is a process which frees people from the fear of want and exploitation. It is a movement away from political, economic, or social oppression. Through development, political independence acquires its true significance. Moreover, it is a process of growth, a movement essentially springing from within the developing society". The UNDP (1991) explains that development is the basic objective of expanding the range of people's choices, making development more democratic and participatory. The UNDP (1991) further emphasised that these options should include access to income and opportunities, education and health, as well as a clean and safe physical environment. Development is the process of removing constraints that hinder the satisfaction of group needs. These constraints include, among other things, physical, economic, and socio-political constraints, as well as those addressed through policy development, strategies, and plans. There are other types of development, such as legal, political, engineering, economic, industrial, and administrative development.

The economist is inclined to say that development is the process whereby a given society's real per capita income increases over a long period, subject to the stipulation that the number below an "absolute poverty line" does not become unequal. A sustained increase in real income is significant from the development standpoint, not simply a short-period rise, such as during the upswing of the business cycle (Chenery et al., 1974). Myradal (1957) is of the view that "economic development" is an "upward movement of the entire social system, or it may be interpreted as the attainment of several ideals of modernisation". Development can be defined as an increase in productivity, social and economic growth, the acquisition of modern knowledge, the improvement of institutions, the creation of infrastructure, and the enhancement of attitudes. The development includes a logically coordinated system of policy measures and strategic plans that address undesirable conditions in the social and economic systems, thereby removing the factors that have perpetuated a state of underdevelopment and promoting social and economic growth.

To the agriculturist, development is nothing but the development of agricultural resources to boost agricultural productivity in any given society. Engineers will always view development as the creation of facilities that enhance the meaning of life, especially in the landscape. The politician would think of development as it relates to the countryside, encompassing the provision of social and basic amenities such as water, hospitals, primary schools, and electricity. The interrelationships among these various types of development are significant for national, state, and rural economic development. Development can be summarised as enhancing citizens' capacity and capabilities, seizing opportunities in the economic space, and promoting human rights and freedom. Development should be centred around the lives of the citizens.

2.1.3 Rural Development

The concept of rural development has been discussed extensively over the years, accompanied by controversies and disagreements. Its meaning perhaps reflects the various disciplines in rural development planning or studies. Rural Development means different things to different people. There is yet no consensus as to what constitutes "Rural Development". Academicians, Professionals, and policymakers have tried to define it differently to suit their ideological differences. This divergence stems from multifaceted and multidimensional rural development (Davidson, 1981). The OECD (2003) questioned whether development in rural areas was a territorial or sectoral issue, highlighting that it was a location-based question, rather than a theoretical discussion. However, rural development is both territorial and sector-based. It is not an object of one-sided development. It should be a holistic form of development that encompasses all forms of development; it is only in this way that rural development can be made sustainable.

There is a consensus that the rural poor, although poor, possess indigenous intelligence, knowledge, and resources, and, as such, rural development programmes should aim to enable them to develop and utilise these resources and potentials at their disposal rather than being "patronising programmes" (Mabogunje, 1968). In keeping with this, he emphasises that the implication is that "in pursuing any rural development programmes, the rural masses should be taken into confidence and involved sufficiently at all stages for all purposes in order to tap these resources which are their exclusive preserve. Ajaegbu (1977) conceives of rural development as not merely agricultural growth alone, but as the creation and fair sharing of social and economic benefits resulting from growth. This is supported by Irwin et al. (2010, p. 523), who state that "rural areas have seen improved rural-urban income parity, farm population decline, and significant rural economic diversification" in the past decades. The rural areas have undergone significant transformations through massive efforts to increase production, create and spread employment opportunities, and address the fundamental causes of poverty and illiteracy. It will help establish an economic base that generates progressively higher levels of production and living.

Rural development empowers rural people and encourages rural communities to utilise their indigenous resources within their domain through technological means and innovations, supported by private and public investment and assistance, to manage their development. Rural development unleashes human potential, intuition, and innovation by promoting social and economic values, such as providing healthcare, education facilities, infrastructure, and services that inspire people to work hard and encourage informed decision-making at the local level.

Polices and strategies for rural development are created and put into practice to boost social and economic growth in rural areas, while also supporting national economic development and overall growth. Nicolaides & Dludla (2023) state that to stimulate rural development, the Department of Rural Development and Land Reform (DRDLR) is authorised to initiate, facilitate, coordinate, catalyse, and implement an integrated rural development programme to create vibrant, equitable, and sustainable social and economic rural communities. It further implicates the distinct features of rural development: mobilisation and equitable allocation of resources, participation, economic production, and integration.

The primary challenge of rural development in Africa is the lack of rural community participation in strategic development and implementation. This challenge has led to a high level of rural-to-urban migration due to the unsustainable nature of rural development caused by holistic methods that involve public participation. Furthermore, it has led to frustration and economic hardship for many urban dwellers who are unable to return to their rural areas after experiencing economic misfortune, such as job loss or business closure. Rural development has long been a neglected aspect of the overall planning process; attention has primarily been directed at urban containment and nationwide protection rather than ensuring proper rural development, which is essential for sustainable economic development and national growth.

In Africa, many national governments have emphasised their commitment to sustainable agricultural and rural development through various programmes; these programmes will be examined in Chapter Three of this book, "Policies and Strategies of Rural Development". South Africa has some of the best rural development policies, strategies, and programmes; however, implementing these programmes has become cumbersome. Many other African countries lack commitment to rural development, and some do not have proper, holistic rural development plans to encourage sustainable social and economic growth. The concern for rural development is rooted in the fact that rural development planning is essential for achieving balanced national economic development, as a large proportion of the African population resides in rural areas.

2.1.4 Africa's Rural Economy and Population

Successful planning of rural development leads to the development of the rural economy. A rural economy could be driven informally when it is not planned and coordinated; it is organic and found in many parts of Africa. When it is planned through proper rural development planning, it becomes formal and organised, linked to formal market systems, and tends to benefit many rural populations more than when it is organic and not formally planned. A rural economy comprises the social, economic, and financial systems of rural communities. Rural economy features also include employment opportunities, means of income, wages, and social services that impact the overall economic development of the rural settlements. Whether planned or organic, a rural economy provides opportunities for social and economic engagements that provide productive jobs, poverty alleviation, food safety, and an improved standard of living. Unfortunately, despite the significant role of the rural economy, decent work is limited, with most people living in poverty in rural areas of Africa.

The rural economy encompasses a range of activities, including commercial, agricultural, craft, cultural, small-scale mining, and agricultural production, in rural areas. It is a significant foundation for the employment and livelihood strategies of rural people, whether in the formal or informal rural economy. A rural economy provides and produces what it consumes as a source of income, and the types of natural resources drive it in rural areas, particularly in organic rural economies. The type of rural economy is examined in Fig. 2.2 below, highlighting the percentages of the rural population engaged in the rural economy and the types of economy in which they are involved.

World Bank (….) reveals that the rural population of Africa in 2023 is 718,293,979. The total population of Africa is about 1.4 billion. Furthermore, the data in Fig. 1 above reveal that most African people practise informal farming. Similarly, most of the informal farmers live in rural areas. According to Galal (2024), in 2023, the portion of people living in rural areas in Africa dropped to nearly 55 per cent. He further highlighted that since the commencement of the twenty-first century, the share of the rural population in the total population has followed a declining trend. The decline in the rural population can be attributed to rural-to-urban migration, mainly due to the lack of rural development. However, the percentage of the rural population is higher than that of the urban population. Nevertheless, the rural economy remains unplanned, mainly, with many rural economies operating organically.

For the past two decades, many African countries have prioritised the urban economy over the rural economy. Additionally, the government's neglect of rural

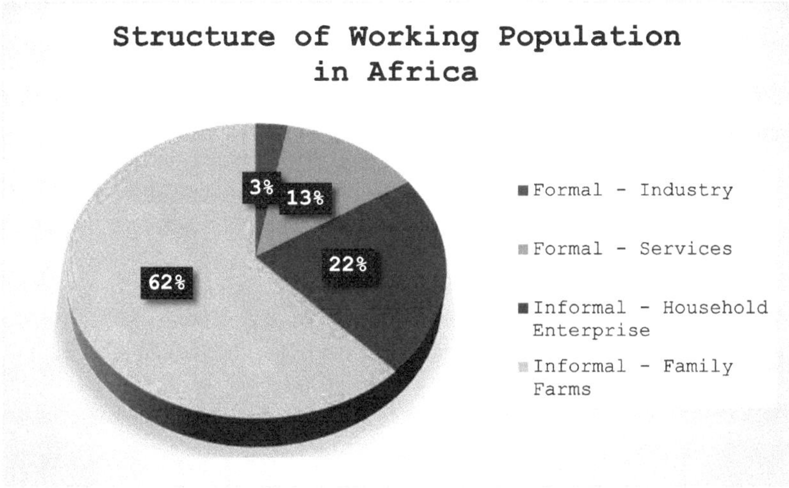

Fig. 2.2 Structure of the Working Population in Africa *Source* FAO 2015

areas in its plans leads to rural graduates from higher institutions migrating to urban areas in search of a better future due to the lack of rural economic planning and growth. These new graduates, mainly young and urban-driven, tend to see no economic future in rural areas. Thus, spatial and economic planning for rural areas should be of paramount importance. Spatial economic planning of rural areas will appeal to young people and draw them back to rural areas, encouraging them to stay due to the equal economic and social opportunities available in urban areas. The rural population data and its implications underscore the importance of rural development, particularly in Africa, where most of the population resides in rural settlements. Hence, rural economic diversification through inclusive rural development planning has significant potential to reduce rural poverty, increase agricultural production, and enhance investments in businesses, industries, and small, medium, and micro enterprises (SMMEs), thereby advancing the food and livelihood security of rural households. It will also encourage many rural graduates to seek jobs or start their businesses in rural areas and attract some urban youths to rural areas due to the sustainable economic opportunities.

2.1.5 Rural Economic Growth and Economic Development

There are differences between economic development and economic growth, although many people assume they are the same. Economic development is about improving people's lives, including their living standards and overall well-being, by creating and expanding economic activities, vital services, and infrastructure. Economic growth focuses on increasing an economy's output (like GDP), such as an increase in people's or the population's income. The Differences between the two are broken down in Table 2.1 below.

Economic development aims to improve a country's population's overall quality of life and well-being, encompassing economic, social, and political aspects. It improves literacy rates, life expectancy, access to healthcare, and other qualitative measures that improve the quality of life of rural people. Todaro and Smith (2015) define economic development as the enhancement of productivity potential, improvement in the quality of life, and increased employment levels that lead to sustainable and inclusive economic growth, resulting in short-term GDP growth. Kane and Sand (1988) explain that economic development enhances the regional economy's ability to generate wealth for all local inhabitants. Then, the United Nations (2015 B) asserts that the Human Development Index (HDI) summarises the measure of typical achievement dimensions of human development and is an accepted tool for measuring economic development.

Economic growth focuses primarily on increasing the production of goods and services within an economy, often measured by GDP growth. It examines the increased manufacturing, agricultural, and business outputs that affect economic growth. These outputs could yield more if there is robust economic development, such as infrastructure development and other social facilities. Dollar and Kraay

Table 2.1 Difference between Economic Growth and Development

Item	Economic Development	Economic Growth
Time	Long term	Short term
Goal	Improve overall quality of life and well-being.	Increase production and income.
Focus	Qualitative improvements in living standards and well-being.	Quantitative increase in output.
Indicators	Rate of literacy, access to infrastructure, health, education, and other social services that improve lives.	It is measured by gross domestic product.

Source Author 2025

(2001) state that economic growth could lead to poverty reduction by raising the incomes of everyone in society, including the poor. In differentiating between economic growth and development, Haller (2012) states that the primary distinction lies in the scope of each concept. Economic growth focuses on quantitative activities within the economy, whereas economic development encompasses a broader range, encompassing both economic growth and qualitative structural changes in the economy and society.

2.1.6 Inclusive Rural Development Planning

Rural development planning enhances the value of life and social and economic security for people living in rural areas (Moseley, 2003). Inclusive rural development is anchored in a holistic approach to rural development that encompasses all sectors of social and economic development and growth. Inclusive rural development further facilitates the identification of rural or local resources and potentials for rural development planning, which raises questions such as what kind of rural development planning or project to embark upon. The identification of these resources and potential could be beneficial for inclusive rural development if the risks in rural areas are identified and mitigated. Rural development planning that fails to incorporate an inclusive approach involving rural communities is likely to be unsuccessful. Rural development planning becomes realistic when rural communities and people who intend to participate in the process of infrastructural development are involved. Inclusive rural development aims to create favourable conditions for developing rural areas and their resources to support economic activities. Inclusive rural development should provide opportunities for the poor, women, youths, vulnerable individuals, and minority groups. Inclusive rural development should address the issue of income inequality between rural and urban areas. The United Nations (2021) states that inclusive rural development requires localised rural policies and actions at the national level, as well as the right mix of economic and social policies at both the rural and national levels, to spur economic development while reducing poverty and inequality in rural areas.

Planning for inclusive rural development emphasises the need for social and economic justice. It implies that people should be involved from the start, as they will define the needs and aspirations of rural communities based on their own needs, goals, and vision for the area. However, most rural development policies and strategic planners often overlook the basic knowledge and understanding of rural settings, which is vital for every stage of planning rural development plans and initiatives. Kosiedovskyi (2016) indicated that inclusive development is a pattern of development that unites society in compliance with the ideals and ideologies of human rights, provides people with opportunities to participate in social and economic existence, and ensures the participation of communities and accountability for the adoption and implementation of decision-making. Kosiedovskyi further stated that the definition is based on scientific publications and the provisions of the UNDP and World Bank documents. Therefore, Inclusive development plans ensure comprehensive rural planning processes and provide opportunities for poor people to gain economic development and growth opportunities.

Enhancing rural development projects through effective, inclusive planning is one of the greatest challenges confronting rural and local economic development. Nhlakanipho (2010) noted that the rural poor have not taken advantage of the enormous development efforts of the last three decades in proportion to their needs. Unless rural communities are given opportunities to participate in rural development interventions and plans designed to improve their living conditions, the spatial inequalities between urban and rural areas will continue to increase. Furthermore, an inclusive rural transformation is to be achieved through rural settlement dwellers taking an active role in shaping solutions to the social and economic challenges.

2.1.7 Sustainable Rural Development

Sustainable rural development is a comprehensive strategy that seeks to harmonise economic growth, social and cultural activities, and environmental concerns within the framework of rural development and spatial planning. Its core is to ensure the eternal improvement of the quality of life for current and future generations by creating rational proportions between various types of capital—economic, human, social, and natural capital (Borys, 2016). "Sustainable Agricultural and Rural Development (SARD) is considered an essential step toward achieving the first Millennium Development Goal (MDG) of eradicating extreme hunger and poverty" (Sumelius et al., 2009, p. 8). Sumelius et al. (2009) suggested that to improve the SARD, cooperation, trade, and agricultural policy should be implemented to enhance agriculture's contribution to economic development and poverty reduction. Some of the most significant challenges to sustainable rural development include population growth, which can lead to hunger and poverty, as well as skyrocketing energy prices in many African countries, resulting in high food prices. According to Nicolaides and Dludla (2023), they state that sustainable rural development deals with a range of issues, including reform, access to land use, management, and transformation of land relations and other matters associated with the hopes and lifestyles of those who live on the land and who depend on it for their livelihoods. Nicolaides and Dludla (2023) opined that sustainable strategic goals should support and drive initiatives to inter alia:

1. Adopt applicable land reform and land restitution programmes.
2. Implement sustainable land reform through access to and productive use of land.
3. Guarantee spatial equity through successful land planning and administration.
4. Restructuring the policy, legislative, and institutional environment.
5. Enhance food production and access to affordable and diverse food options.
6. Improve rural services to strengthen sustainable rural livelihoods.
7. Improve access to employment and skills development.
8. Improve institutional measures for efficient cooperative governance, stakeholder participation, and service quality.

A sustainable rural development strategy must incorporate innovation dimensions to support economic growth that is inclusive and transformative for marginalised, poor, and underdeveloped rural communities (Papaioannou, 2014; Swaans et al., 2014; Phiri et al., 2016).

UNDP (2022) emphasised that sustainable rural development is vital to nations' economic, social, and environmental viability. It is essential for eradicating poverty since global poverty is predominantly rural. UNDP (2022) further specified that indicators of poverty go beyond the urban-rural divide; it has subregional and regional contexts and, therefore, are critical, and there is great value to be gained by coordinating rural development initiatives that contribute to sustainable livelihoods through efforts at the global, regional, national, and local spheres. The above highlights the importance of having an integrated and inclusive rural development that encompasses both regional and urban economies, promoting sustainability. The integration of regional and urban economies with rural areas will narrow the inequalities between urban and rural areas, providing more opportunities for rural settlements.

Connecting urban and rural economies is vital for reducing gaps in infrastructure and preserving rural resources. As a result, investing in rural infrastructure and services is crucial for a sustainable rural future development. UNDP (2022) specified that sustainable rural development will depend on developing and implementing comprehensive strategies for dealing with climate change, drought, desertification, and natural disasters, which include actions on the following:

1. Alleviation of poverty in the rural areas.
2. Initiating policies, strategies, and yearly budgets that are pro-rural sustainable development at the national state and rural sphere.
3. Creating accessibility to services and basic needs of rural settlements to improve livelihood and productive activities.

A. Social protection and empowerment programmes should be established to support vulnerable households, individuals with disabilities, and the unemployed, many of whom reside in rural areas. Actions are needed.

   To build social capital and resilience in rural communities by empowering women, small-scale farmers, and indigenous peoples, including through securing equitable land tenure; access to land, water, financial resources and technologies by women, indigenous peoples and other vulnerable groups; support to technologies; to help rural areas to manage better the various risks they face, including price, weather, climate, water shortages, land degradation natural disasters, and as well as agricultural insurance markets; protect and ensure sustainable use of traditional knowledge; support inclusive participation of rural development plans; plan for the resilience of rural communities to cope with and recover from natural disasters; support labour-intensive economic activities in addition to capital-intensive programmes, training and capacity buildings.
B. To ensure that human capacity in rural areas is strengthened by supporting rural healthcare, education programmes, and facilities; Reduce illiteracy in rural communities and support vocational and entrepreneurship training, access to information, and the promotion of extension services to support sustainable development planning and decision-making.
C. Promote public and private investment in infrastructure and services in rural areas that include roads, waterways and transport systems, storage and market facilities, livestock facilities, irrigation systems, affordable housing, water supply and sanitation services, electrification facilities, renewable energy, and information and communications networks; To support the development of rural organisations, such as community-driven cooperatives, to enhance investment in essential infrastructure and services.

D. Inspire the creation of new jobs and income opportunities in rural settlements by supporting rural diversification; provide suitable land use, entrepreneurial training, credit and other support to off-farm and other non-primary production activities; strengthen linkages between agriculture and other sectors of the rural economy; develop a framework to add value to agricultural products locally, regionally and nationally and, if possibly globally to generate income; to promote sustainable tourism and forest management; promote rural products, finance, micro credit with guarantees and venture capital; promote the development of integration of smallholder family agriculture and sharing of knowledge and superlative practices; promote non-agricultural industries such as mining, service industries, construction and commerce.
E. To ensure the sustainability of the environment through the use of rural resources in a sustainable manner; Support environmentally responsive practices and conserve natural resources through community-based management programmes and projects, promoting environmentally sound waste management practices.
F. Promotion of women's empowerment and gender equality by involving women in decision-making, resource ownership, entrepreneurship, capital, and production activities; promote gender equality in the economic space in all aspects of rural development; and promote the rights of women and the concept of empowerment and gender equality in rural areas.

Sustainable rural development is summarised as empowering the rural settlements and communities through holistic rural development project and programme, ensuring that the environment is protected for future use, and providing infrastructure and services to the rural people that involve them through initiation, planning and management; creating opportunities and jobs that sustainable to the rural population; empowering women youths, and disables; and ensuring that rural development embraces smart cities ideologies. Community participation is the bedrock of rural development (Nekwaya, 2007). Furthermore, community-based rural development lies in the active participation of community members and a robust sustainability plan. Experience from the developed economies has shown that a sound rural development policy must be sustainable, efficient, and affordable. The World Bank (2004) asserts that the present era is characterised by efforts to promote citizens' participation in community development, which necessitates a fundamental shift in attitudes and techniques, thereby encouraging planning with rural communities at the grassroots level.

2.1.8 Current Trend in Rural Development

Over the past decade, many rural areas have shifted their focus from national issues to global trends. New global challenges are now emerging in rural development, particularly access to the internet and mobile phones, which are enabling local communities to reach a wider customer base through online trade. For example, in the village of Ihitteaforukwu Mbaise, Imo State, Nigeria, some young people have found a way to sell their products online to international customers, thanks to the internet and mobile phones available in the rural area. Furthermore, current trends in rural development emphasise inclusive social and economic activities and growth, diversification of the rural economy, and leveraging local resources through initiatives such as Rural Agri-Parks, the promotion of sustainable agriculture, and investment in infrastructure and education to address challenges like poverty and unemployment. The current trend in rural development includes the development and enhancement of rural ecological systems, crafts, and culture to promote tourism activities. Florin and Latu (2020) noted that there have been significant changes in rural development processes and economic approaches, particularly about food security, competitiveness, and territorial development. This change strengthens the rural economy, but it also creates new challenges that require new policies and strategies. EPRS (2017) stated that the issue of rural development is becoming increasingly common as an object of research because it directly concerns the national security of states. Petukhova et al. (2023) gave a direction for new rural development research as indicated in Table 2.2.

Petukhova et al. (2023) expressed that Japan, the United States, Brazil, and China have the largest share in global R&D spending in agriculture, emphasising rural tourism, environmental issues, climate change, social innovation, sustainable development, and eco-settlements.

Those concerned about rural development planning suggest that the new approach is a bottom-up approach. This prioritises community consultation and participation in planning and implementing rural development. The conservative top-down approach to rural development is considered unsustainable (Bakre, 2022). In Nigeria, where the top-down approach still exists, rural development has become unsustainable and, most of the time, a white elephant project. In South Africa, a gradual shift towards bottom-up practices in rural development approaches has occurred over the past decade, driven by policies and strategies, with significant success (Makkonen and Kahila, 2021). Supported the ideology that the bottom-up approach, which supports an inclusive approach to rural

Table 2.2 Directions of R&D depending on the problems of rural areas (from the lowest to the upper level)

No.	Problem	R&D Direction
1	Low level of rural development	Methods of attracting innovation, development of non-agricultural activities, rural construction and healthcare, territorial planning
2	The outflow of the rural population to the city	Mechanisms of attracting the population to rural areas, counter-urbanisation, and rural revival
3	Problems of agricultural production	Mechanisms to support farmers and ensure the availability of food, and rural cooperation
4	Environmental problems	Sustainable rural development and sustainable agriculture, creation of eco-settlements, rural landscape research, and renewable energy sources
5	Climate change	Methods of reducing dependence on natural and climatic factors, mechanisms for dealing with natural disasters
6	The transition of rural areas to the 6.0 technology order	Mechanisms for the introduction of social innovations, digitalisation, and the creation of smart villages

Source Petukhova et al. (2023)

development, promotes holistic and sustainable rural development by leveraging regional resources. Castro-Arce Vanclay (2020) indicate that local authorities should build their strategies on regional resources, involve other local organisations and community members, and integrate different policy sectors in their development initiatives.

Smart rural communities, also known as Smart Villages, are the latest trend. The goal is to use technology and innovation to improve the lives and living standards of people in rural areas. This aims to create social and economic opportunities through innovative technologies and the use of cleaner energies to protect the environment. Zavratnik (2018) states that the concept of urban smart communities is already well established, but less so for rural communities, as the concept of Smart Village has only recently gained momentum. For example, in the EU, the Smart Village Initiative was launched by the European Parliament in 2017. The Sustainable Development in Communities—Indicators for Smart Cities recommends an International Standard to help cities implement smart city policies and build a dynamic and innovative economy ready for the challenges of tomorrow. The same standard can also be applied to rural development, creating Smart

Villages and Smart Rural Settlements. Thus, an increasing number of researchers are discussing the need to develop smart development in rural settlements (Cowie et al. (2020), Park & Cha (2019), and Hosseini et al. (2018).

2.1.9 Theoretical Framework

Theory serves as a foundation for a realistic understanding of a specific sphere of influence. All development theories, including classical, Marxist, and Schumpeterian approaches, are based on logical and systematic processes, albeit in abstract terms. Moreover, modern development theory has often been misinterpreted as a blueprint for successful development, with access to modern economics being seen as a source of new magical powers. However, to tackle the challenges of rural development and economies, practitioners should find ways to utilise these theories to create effective policies, strategies, plans, programmes, and projects.

Researchers have advanced various theories to get to the root of rural issues and challenges. In the works of Svenning (1969), an "adopter categorisation", viewing innovation adoption in rural societies in terms of time adoption, individuals are divided into categories: innovators, early adopters, and early majority. Furthermore, Mijindadi (1978) explained the idea of quick positive results concentrated on an area of "High Growth Potentials", as opposed to those of "Low Growth Potential" and "Future Growth Potential". However, the idea of holistic rural development does not oppose any form of growth, whether high or low potential. All rural areas have potential that can be developed, as well as risks and challenges that can be mitigated, to achieve sustainable rural development. The theoretical concept of High Potentials and Low Potentials is not feasible for holistic rural development and national growth. However, this book will consider three development theories. These are:

1. Integrated Rural Development Theory
2. Economic Base Theory
3. Big Push Theory

2.1.9.1 Integrated Rural Development Theory

Basler and Brunswick (1979) indicated that the concept of Integrated Rural Development (IRD) as a strategy for developing countries has been a focal point of discussion on development policy since the early 1970s. The integrated rural development theory ideology aims to integrate the neglected rural poor into the process of increasing the well-being of the rural population. The process also aimed to apply the interdependent relations of all economic, social, political, and technical factors. Henceforth, any approach to rural development must begin with an evaluation of the current situation and the identification of existing potentials, challenges, and risks. The inclusive integrated rural development theory supports examines and implementation of these factors—agricultural, human resources, social organisation, economic structure, technology and innovation, infrastructure (physical infrastructure, transport and communication, social infrastructure, spatial order), institutions and organisations, and services (marketing, credit extension, social security). In the Therefore, integrated rural development should concentrate on people and the various factors that contribute to potential rural progress. Its most important objectives, as highlighted by Basler and Brunswick (1979), are:

1. Improvement in food production that enhances food accessibility for the population.
2. Advancement of the material infrastructure, training and health accessibility.
3. Provision of agricultural jobs (including complementary services) and non-agricultural fields.
4. Surge in the rural population's employment, productivity, and incomes through improvements in their living circumstances.
5. Integration of the population into socio-economic development and inclusive decision-making.

Thus, while agricultural development does not embrace all the components of integrated rural development, integrated development includes agricultural development. The integrated rural development theory examines the needs of the population within a holistic framework. The rural population needs food, but perhaps more basic than food, they need good health. Additionally, they require schools, amenities such as clean water, a reliable communication system, and electricity. It is also true that the rural population has a farming proportion, but there are also tailors, carpenters, blacksmiths, fishermen, hunters, and traders, among others. The underlying principle behind integrated rural development theory is that there are some measures to improve the living standards and welfare of rural people.

2.1.9.2 Economic Base Theory

The Economic Base Theory posits that a region's success is driven by external demand for its social and economic products and services. This concept applies to rural development planning by recognising and encouraging export-oriented social and economic activities to stimulate development and growth. Krikelas (1992) and Thiebout (1956) described the economic base theory as a theoretical framework that describes the process of local economic development relevant to small regions. It is significant in classifying the economy of a rural community, town or region. Thus, the economic base development theory identifies the fundamental sources of employment and income, providing insight into the overall economic situation.

Philippe and Ruault (2019) state that economic-based theory provides an interesting understanding of regional development from a macroeconomic viewpoint, but there is a need to recognise the impact of day-to-day mobility as a major disruptive factor that is currently the case. Therefore, it signifies the mechanism for identifying local development factors and regional specificities that help shape development policies, resulting in sustainable rural economic growth. The theory could be applied to an analytical method that illustrates many fundamental techniques local and regional planners use, including areal comparisons, local versus regional/national conditions, and standardising values. The economic base theory's significance for rural development relies on identifying potentials that encourage development, support exportation, and bring more income and economic diversification to the rural economy. It provides the necessary linkage to regional and global value chains.

The theory provides the steps to identify the core rural development economic activities that are the primary drivers of income and employment. These primary economic drivers of the economy are linked to the export sectors that will generate income that will be recirculated to the rural economy. To strengthen the ideology of the economic base theory, targeted interventions should be implemented through infrastructural development, agricultural investment, economic diversification, the improvement of indigenous knowledge and resources, and human capital development.

2.1.9.3 Big Push Theory

The theory supports the idea that a certain level of resources must be committed to developing an area to witness sustainable development and economic growth. For example, a certain level of infrastructure development investment is necessary in rural areas to initiate economic growth, leading to job creation, economic empowerment, and increased potential opportunities. The theory supports investment in social and economic infrastructure, as well as manufacturing, in rural areas.

The Big Push Theory is supported by the idea of the Economic Base Theory, which posits that the means of reinforcing and developing the rural economy is to develop and enhance the basic sector. The basic sector is consequently categorised as the "engine" of the rural economy. Hence, this book argues that the Big Push should be adequately understood, and then it will effectively stimulate economic growth in many rural areas of Africa. The Big Push idea is not about allocating resources, but rather about how resources are properly allocated in a transparent and accountable manner to rural development programmes.

The Big Push Theory highlights the importance of expertise among various actors in achieving this goal, including government institutions, private institutions, NGOs, and international organisations. The theory supports government interventions, incentives, and private sector investment that address market failures by investing in the potential of rural areas and mitigating the risks. The Big Push theory can be applied by institutions to identify rural potential and areas where investment is needed, such as transportation, energy, and communication infrastructure. These can create conditions for private sector investment and job creation. Rosenstein (1943) claimed that there were two options to solve rural economic problems: emigration or industrialisation. He further said that emigration was not the answer, but he concluded that the regions must industrialise to absorb labourers into the economy. To push the narrative of the positive impact of Big Push, Rorenstein (1943) indicated that the least amount of resources must be allocated to break the initial inertia, as a certain amount of speed is required for an aircraft to be airborne. In furtherance of this, Murphy et al. (1989) and Kremer (1993) stated that returns to investment in skills are low if skills fail to capitalise on economies of scale or production complementarities. Therefore, it becomes essential that investments comprehend the value chain of an industry sector to propel that sector towards self-sustaining growth. Hence, the Big Push theory provides a framework for understanding how investment, infrastructure, and coordination can work together to promote rural economic development.

3 Africa and Rural Development Infrastructure Status Quo

Abstract

This chapter explores Africa's infrastructure development and its importance for alleviating poverty, creating jobs, and empowering youth, particularly in rural areas. Despite vast resources, poor infrastructure limits industrial growth, leads to exporting unprocessed resources, and hampers economic potential. Africa requires billions of dollars annually to bridge the significant infrastructure gap, which will shape the continent's infrastructural demands. Infrastructure deficits hinder productivity, GDP growth, and access to education, healthcare, and transportation. Investing in quality infrastructure is essential to reaching the SDGs and Agenda 2063.

In sub-Saharan Africa, infrastructure is critically underdeveloped, and the majority of the population lacks access to basic infrastructure, which hinders access and poor infrastructure deters investment, especially in rural areas.

Furthermore, fundings come from governments, international institutions, and private partnerships, but challenges like poor planning, corruption, and political interference hinder progress. Strengthening regulation, transparency, and public-private partnerships are crucial. Better infrastructure will benefit rural areas, boost trade, and promote industrialisation. Addressing the infrastructure gap requires investment, planning, and good governance for sustainable, inclusive development.

C. Osuigwe, *Economic Development of Rural Areas*, Sustainable Development Goals Series, https://doi.org/10.1007/978-3-032-10572-1_3

3.1 Introduction

For Africa to eradicate poverty, create the necessary jobs for young people, and empower them to reach their full potential, sustainable rural development is vital. To make this development truly effective, rural areas need to be revitalised, and robust territorial spatial planning must be implemented to drive social and economic growth. Achieving these goals requires a joint effort to upgrade infrastructure, including energy, water, sanitation, electricity, and roads. There should be a significant improvement in access to quality education and healthcare, alongside advancements in various modes of transportation, communication systems, and an increase in indigenous knowledge and sustainable ecosystems. The African Development Bank estimated that Africa's infrastructure requires approximately $130–170 billion per year, with a financing gap ranging from $68 to $108 billion (ADB, 2023). This amount underscores the pressing need for infrastructural development in Africa, with the situation being particularly dire in rural areas.

Africa's industrialisation and rural growth have been hampered by inadequate infrastructure development. As a result, the continent's resources are mainly exported in their raw state, rather than being processed into finished products. This has a considerable impact on tapping the potential of rural areas that could help drive the continent's economic growth.

The positive impact of infrastructure on productivity has a significant influence on social and economic development and growth. Additionally, the increase in infrastructure development has a positive impact on GDP growth. Infrastructure also has a ripple effect, reducing the costs of transactions and other inputs needed for production. When electricity is inadequate or unavailable, it drives up production costs. No manufacturer wants to generate their electricity due to the high associated costs. Furthermore, no business wants to set up in an area without access to goods, services, and transportation, as poor roads lead to sharply increased transportation costs, ultimately affecting productivity and overall costs. The same applies to water and communications. These factors add additional costs to production. High-quality infrastructure is indispensable for Africa to achieve the Sustainable Development Goals (SDGs), the African Union's Agenda 2063, and the African Development Bank's (AfDB) High Five Goals. Furthermore, infrastructure development in rural areas is particularly significant, considering that the majority of the African population resides in these areas. Therefore, it is crucial to examine the factors that shape rural infrastructure development and their associated conditions.

3.1.1 State of Africa Infrastructure

Sub-Saharan Africa's primary development challenge remains the lack of physical infrastructure. Many of Africa's essential infrastructure sectors remain relatively underdeveloped. Lui (2024) states that approximately 60% of people in sub-Saharan Africa still lack electricity, and the transport sector is no exception, with only 25% of roads being paved. This situation restricts trade between African countries and hinders rural development that could have enhanced the value of trade among Africans. Trade among Africans remains below 20%, primarily due to inadequate infrastructure, especially in roads, transport, and communication systems. In terms of telecommunications, mobile phone penetration stood at 44% as of 2022; however, broadband internet coverage remains limited, with only 29% of sub-Saharan Africa having access to the internet (Lui, 2024). These highlight the severity of the financial gap between demand and the current state of infrastructure in Africa. These issues have further deterred investors from conducting business in Africa, particularly in rural areas where infrastructure development is lacking. Many investors would be interested in doing business in rural areas but struggle to access adequate infrastructure and rural markets, particularly because of poor infrastructure.

The data in Table 3.1 below illustrate the rate of infrastructural development in Africa.

According to the Africa Infrastructure Development Index 2018, as shown in Table 3.1, more than 83% of African countries rank below 40% in infrastructural development. Table 3.1 reveals that the top ten countries ranking above 40% are Seychelles, Egypt, Libya, South Africa, Mauritius, Tunisia, Morocco, Algeria, and Cabo Verde, while the rest rank below 40%. Despite the oil boom in Nigeria over the past few years, its ranking is 22.3%. The countries most affected, with rankings below 10%, include Sierra Leone, Ethiopia, the Democratic Republic of Congo, Chad, Somalia, Madagascar, Niger, Eritrea, South Sudan, and the Central African Republic.

Travelling across Africa shows just how bad the state of most roads is, especially in rural areas. Most roads are unpaved and cannot be used during the rainy seasons. The poor condition of roads, particularly in rural areas, cuts off settlements from vital services such as education, healthcare, and various social and economic opportunities. The effects of poor infrastructure are evident in the lack of electricity and frequent power outages in many African countries. Dethier (2015) states that more than 640 million Africans lack access to energy, and electricity accessibility is only 40 per cent, the lowest of all continents. Access

Table 3.1 The Composite Africa Infrastructure Development Index 2018

Country	Percentage	Country	Percentage	Country	Percentage
Seychelles	94.324	Zimbabwe	24.518	Sudan	15.404
Egypt	85.847	Djibouti	24.461	Burundi	15.112
Libya	81.413	Comoros	23.500	Guinea	14.789
South Africa	78.527	Nigeria	22.365	Liberia	14.485
Mauritius	76.787	Zambia	22.289	Guinea-Bissau	13.536
Tunisia	68.982	Cote d'Ivoire	21.960	Togo	12.971
Morocco	64.884	Malawi	21.018	Tanzania	12.543
Algeria	55.793	Rwanda	20.768	Mozambique	12.495
Cabo Verde	47.955	Uganda	20.622	Central African	11.951
Botswana	36.793	Cameroon	19.813	Madagascar	10.734
Gabon	30.670	Angola	19.038	Sierra Leone	9.943
Ghana	28.835	Equatorial Guinea	18.215	Ethiopia	9.699
Namibia	28.652	Congo. Rep.	17.531	Eritrea	8.217
Gambia	28.612	Burkina Faso	17.055	Congo. Dem. Rep.	8.148
São Tomé	27.143	Benin	16.228	Chad	7.239
Senegal	25.965	Mauritania	16.050	Niger	5.508
Swaziland	25.764	Lesotho	16.008	South Sudan	4.603
Kenya	25.604	Mali	15.948	Somalia	3.362

Source AFDB 2018

to energy in rural areas is crucial for development, unlocking economic opportunities and creating jobs. Energy accessibility is also vital for quality health and education, as the effective and efficient administration of these services relies on energy.

Energy and roads are the major drivers of sustainable, inclusive economic growth. Despite Africa's geographical location and access to abundant sunlight and water, the development of renewable energy has been a significant challenge. The data below show the rate of infrastructural development in Africa when compared to the rest of the continent.

Table 3.2 demonstrates that Africa has a disadvantage compared to other continents in access to basic infrastructure and infrastructure that supports economic growth. Only 46 percent of Africa's population has access to electricity, 39 per cent have access to sanitation, and 69 per cent have access to water. This situation is discouraging for both human and economic development. It highlights the urgent need for improvements, especially in rural areas that lack adequate infrastructure and have limited access.

Table 3.3 also reveals Africa's disappointing performance among developing countries. It takes 96.6 days to get a telephone line, compared to 27.5 days in other developing countries. Furthermore, there are 28.1 days of telephone outages per year, compared to 9.1 days in other countries. Furthermore, firms in Africa are more likely to maintain their energy sources than those in other developing countries. These findings highlight the poor infrastructure accessibility and development in Africa, which is particularly pronounced in rural areas.

Improving Africa's infrastructure will significantly benefit the development of rural areas and boost trade and services within the region. It will also enable rural communities to tap into their vast resources for economic growth, benefiting not only their countries but the entire continent. Africa's rural resources are vital for

Table 3.2 Infrastructure access data for selected global regions

Indicators	Africa	Asia	Europe	Latin America
Transport				
Paved road density (km of paved road per 100 km2 of land area	2	29	122	3
Railway lines (km)	46, 380	197, 610	85, 986	89, 002
Information and communication technology				
Fixed broadband subscriptions per 100 population	1	6	15	9
Mobile cellular subscriptions per 100 population	73	85	119	115
Power				
Electricity production per capita (kWh)	572	1, 930	3, 355	2, 116
Electricity access (% of total population)	46	88	100	97
Water Supply and Sanitation				
Improved water (% of total population)	69	90	99	94
Improved sanitation (% of total population)	39	61	93	82

Source AfDB statistics and World Bank WDI database *Note* Data are for 2013.

Table 3.3 Impact of unreliable infrastructure services on the productive sector

Service Problem	Sub-Saharan Africa	Developing Countries
Electricity		
Delay in obtaining electricity connection (days)	79.9	27.5
Electrical outages (days a year)	90.9	28.7
Value of lost output due to electrical outages (per cent of turnover)	6.1	4.4
Firms maintaining their generation equipment (per cent of total)	47.5	31.8
Telecommunications		
Delay in obtaining telephone line (days)	96.6	43
Telephone outages (days a year)	28.1	9.1

Source World Bank 2014

industrial development, enabling sustainable participation in regional and global value chains. However, these resources are still being exported in their raw state, without having a substantial impact on the economic growth of rural Africa. By reducing the export of raw resources and instead focusing on production activities, Africa could see a significant shift towards industrialisation, particularly in rural areas where most of these resources are found.

Nevertheless, funding for infrastructure is a significant burden for many African governments, particularly the poorer nations. Therefore, there is a need for substantial investment in Africa's infrastructure. This investment needs public and private partnerships (PPPs) to be realised. Given the overstretched resources in Africa, it is unlikely that African governments could achieve this alone. Over the past two decades, public and private investment has contributed to some infrastructural development in Africa, particularly in Nigeria and South Africa. However, this investment has had little impact in rural areas, as many investments are concentrated in urban areas or their peripheries. One sector that has attracted public-private partnerships (PPPs) is mobile network infrastructure. However, this has not had a significant impact on the rural population. While many in rural areas have mobile network coverage, they often lack the means to purchase cell phones or smartphones that enable internet access. Figure 3.1 illustrates the internet coverage, connection, and usage gap in Sub-Saharan Africa.

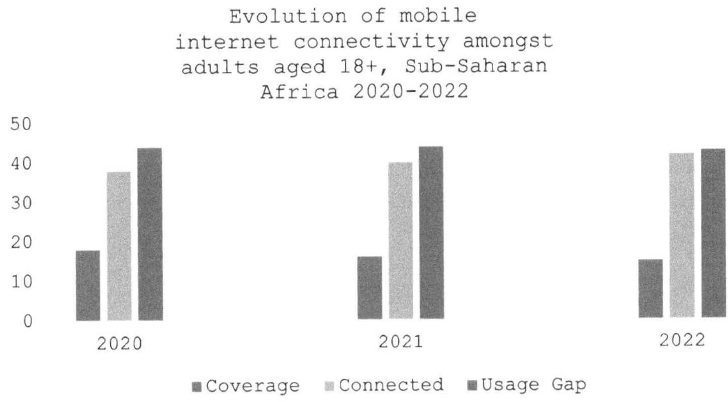

Fig. 3.1 Evolution of mobile internet connectivity amongst adults aged 18+, Sub-Saharan Africa 2020–2022 (*Source* GSMA Intelligence *Base*Adult Population Aged 18 and above)

A coverage gap refers to not being covered by the internet and having no internet connection. The usage gap means that coverage is present but not connected, while the population is connected to mobile internet.

The data in Fig. 3.1 indicate low internet coverage in Africa, despite a high level of coverage as indicated by the usage gap. From 2020 to 2022, the usage gap was very high. This is more prevalent in rural areas due to low-income levels and high unemployment rates. Bridging the internet gap in rural areas will empower smaller businesses and other forms of businesses; it will encourage ideas for business startups.

For PPP to succeed in infrastructure development, African governments are ideally placed to lead the strategy, as they are familiar with deploying resources and identifying areas that require specific types of infrastructure, provided the government is impartial. It is essential to discuss rural development, but it is another matter to say we are prepared to implement it in a sustainable manner. No investor wants to invest in a place where they are not sure of getting their money back, as well as a profit. Unbiased decisions, incorruptible officials, accountability, and transparency are required to make a successful and attractive investment in infrastructure and PPP. Investment in infrastructure, industrial opportunities, commercial activities, and agricultural development in rural areas bolsters potential and hastens inclusive rural development.

3.1.2 Factors Affecting Infrastructure Development in Africa

This chapter examines the current state of infrastructure development in Africa. It has explored some of the challenges faced by rural areas and the crucial role of infrastructure in driving rural development. The following section will examine the reasons behind Africa's underdeveloped infrastructure, particularly in rural areas.

3.1.2.1 Legal and Organisational System

Legal and organisational systems and frameworks influence rural development and planning. They also affect the rights and entitlements of the rural population, which impact their daily livelihoods. Legal and organisational systems are essential foundations for government commitments, accountability, and the long-term sustainability of rural development. Many people living in rural areas are left without a voice and pushed to the sidelines due to their limited involvement in social, economic, and political activities, which further erodes their social, economic, civil, and political rights. Poverty involves a range of deprivations tied to the fundamental aspects of human existence and well-being. The implementation of economic, social, and cultural rights is pivotal in combating poverty (Alston, 2005).

The regulatory frameworks and ineffective institutions or corrupt institutions are significant obstacles to infrastructure development in many African countries, particularly in rural areas. Many African countries' feeble regulatory and institutional capacity encumbers infrastructure development by creating ambiguity for investors, thereby preventing the private sector from partaking in rural development. The impact of a poor institutional and regulatory framework on infrastructure development includes a lack of transparency and accountability, which leads to corruption and the misallocation of funds. Take, for instance, planning for a new township establishment in South Africa, which can take anywhere from 2 to 5 years or even longer. What does this mean? It delays infrastructure development, and service delivery delays investment and development. In Nigeria, for instance, poor regulations and weak institutions have facilitated corruption, as well as the misallocation of funds for infrastructural development.

One of the primary challenges facing Africa's infrastructure development is the shortage of technical and professional expertise in many institutions responsible for planning and implementing these projects. Insufficient or limited professional expertise can lead to suboptimal designs and delays in infrastructure development.

Limited expertise makes it challenging to secure proper funding for infrastructure development, thereby hindering the establishment of a robust regulatory system that supports effective and efficient infrastructure development. Van De Waldt (2014) noted that infrastructure development in Africa is often hindered by poor planning, low operational capacity, corruption, inadequate maintenance, and adverse environmental impacts. It expresses poor institutional and weak regulatory systems that impact the planning and implementation of infrastructural projects. Hence, weak institutions and poorly developed regulatory frameworks lead to a lack of private investment in infrastructure development, delays in infrastructure implementation, poor contract management that results in project stoppages and stagnation, and inadequate project evaluation and monitoring.

Despite these challenges, strengthening the regulatory and institutional framework will lead to sustainable infrastructural development. This can be achieved through transparency and accountability, promoting good governance, enforcing anti-corruption measures in the infrastructure sector, and creating attractive and sustainable conditions for private and public partnerships in infrastructural development. These will foster economic growth and improve the lives of people in rural areas in African countries.

3.1.2.2 Flaws in Infrastructure Planning and Project Organisation

Planning and preparing infrastructure requires a considerable amount of data, information, and stakeholder involvement. Challenges emerge during the initiation, planning, and preparation phases, including inadequate stakeholder engagement throughout all stages, insufficient data collection or a lack of data, inadequate feasibility studies, poor risk management, inadequate budget allocation or a lack of financial understanding, unclear project scope and required expertise, and inadequate environmental impact assessments. These disruptions have affected infrastructure delivery, and their implications have impacted infrastructure planning and processes, resulting in insufficient infrastructure development in rural areas. Khumalo et al. (2017) state that for government organisations to save money, there should be appropriate infrastructural planning concurrently with effective and efficient monitoring and evaluation. Leigland and Roberts (2007) indicated that the project planning process has been more challenging to accomplish than the projected development of many major infrastructure projects in Africa. During the planning processes for infrastructural development, it is essential to determine the sufficiency of data required to develop sustainable infrastructure planning. At this stage, community needs and gaps are assessed and established. All the stakeholders should be identified and engaged to reduce project conflicts and disruptions.

During the planning stage, it is essential to clarify the project goals, deliverables, and scope of work to avoid unsustainable infrastructural development. These will help create detailed designs, specs, budgets, and timeframes. In this phase, not identifying risks and struggling to mitigate them can hold up the rollout of an infrastructure project. Therefore, risk plans and management should be developed. In furtherance of these, the need for qualified experts is very significant; they should be able to provide professional advice and planning for infrastructural development. The major challenge in Africa is nepotism, where leaders often appoint individuals close to them to lead projects, and many of these projects ultimately fail. Therefore, the need for good resources and capacity should be one of the most significant values needed for sustainable infrastructural development. African governments and International Financial Institutions (IFIs) need to engage in medium- and long-term infrastructure planning, informed by sufficient data on demographics and development objectives.

3.1.2.3 Governance and Corruption

Governance, transparency, and accountability are essential factors that guarantee the success of rural development's infrastructural planning and execution. The lack of accountability, transparency, and good governance results in corruption. It significantly impedes infrastructure development through the misallocation of funds, inflated infrastructure budgets, a lack of investor confidence, and delays in completing infrastructural projects. One of the significant obstacles to infrastructure development is corruption, which occurs when funds allocated for infrastructure development are diverted to personal use through cronies and relatives. There is also a lack of oversight due to poor transparency, which enables corruption in infrastructure development through contractors' inflation of prices with the backing of corrupt government and organisational staff. Some of the factors hindering rural infrastructural development include kickbacks to facilitate contract awards, the inflation of material costs with the assistance of contractors, and fictitious infrastructural projects created to divert funds from the public purse.

Politics have been instrumental in Africa, alongside social and economic factors that determine the placement of projects. In many African countries, the construction of roads, development of airports and seaports, and siting of power plants and small to medium-sized enterprise (SMME) projects are often driven by political considerations rather than thorough social and economic feasibility studies. For example, Nigeria has the capacity to develop five seaports across three regions (Southeast, South-South, and South-West Regions) in a sustainable manner. However, due to political and ethnic hegemony, Nigeria has only two functional seaports in one state (Lagos), resulting in delays in exports and imports, and increased costs on goods and services that affect all areas of development, particularly in rural areas. Many projects in Africa turn into white elephants; some fail, while others become unsustainable due to political decisions rather than social and economic factors. Political decisions often favour building new projects over optimising or renovating existing ones. In 2024, Peter Obi questioned the Tinibu-led government's decision to award a contract for the new coastal road at a cost of 9.8 billion dollars, instead of repairing damaged national roads across Nigeria. It was revealed that the company that awarded the contract had Tinibu's son as a director.

Africa's infrastructure challenge, especially in rural areas, is holding back economic growth and development. A shortfall in infrastructure is evident when constructing new infrastructure and maintaining existing facilities. Many old or newly built infrastructures are poorly maintained, resulting in damage and potential reconstruction costs that would be more expensive and inefficient use of public funds. These have consequences for the economy and create a burden on infrastructure utilities, which could lead to rundown facilities and the provision of low-quality infrastructure. For instance, in Imo State, Nigeria, the former governor, Rochas Okorocha, embarked on building hospitals in all the local governments of the state. These include local governments located in rural areas. He failed to complete the hospital projects, and the reasons are best known to him. All the unfinished hospital buildings have been damaged, and public resources have been wasted. To tackle these challenges, African countries need to establish transparent systems that promote public disclosure of contracts and thorough feasibility studies. Governments and organisations should train their staff on ethics and the impact of corruption on the public's overall welfare and the economy.

3.1.3 Sources of Infrastructure in Africa

This book explores the scope of infrastructural challenges and the factors contributing to them in Africa. It is also essential to investigate the sources of infrastructure development in Africa. According to the African Development Bank (ADB), Africa is estimated to require USD 130–170 billion per year in infrastructure financing, which translates to an annual deficit of USD 68–108 billion (AFDB, 2023). Is this money available? Who finances Africa's infrastructural development? There are numerous sources of infrastructure development finance in Africa, which have implications for rural development. The sources of finance for infrastructure development in Africa are demonstrated in Fig. 3.2.

The primary funders of infrastructure in Africa can be categorised into three groups.

1. Government (National, State, and Local Government)
2. Banks (International, Regional, and Local),
3. NGOs, and

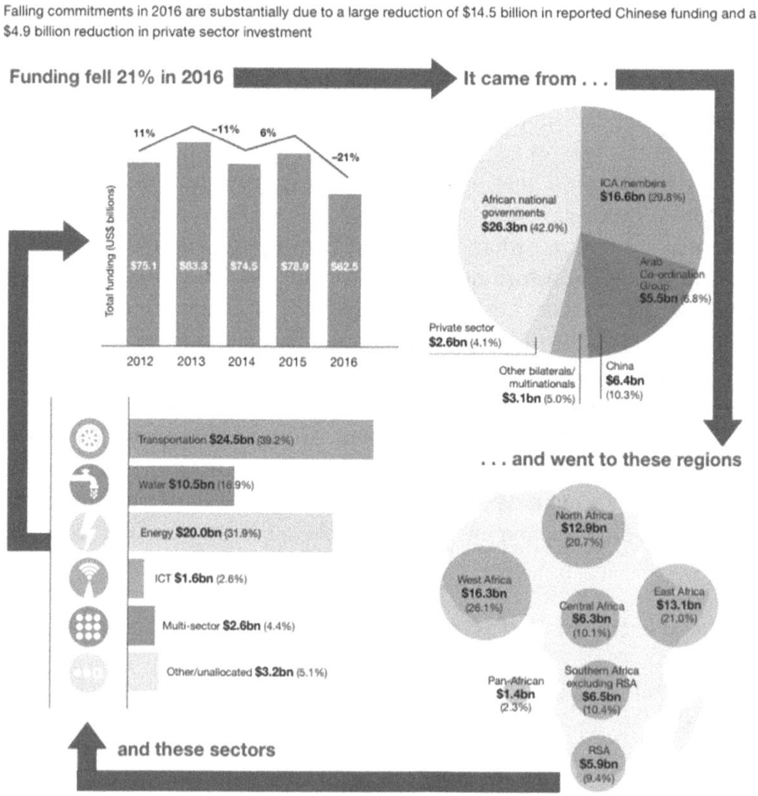

Fig. 3.2 Source of Infrastructure Funding in Africa *Source* AFDB 2019

4. International Institutions.

Figure 3.2 above suggests that African governments are the main funders of infrastructure development. However, this may not be entirely accurate in some poorer African countries that rely heavily on international funding for infrastructure development. According to Thusi and Mlambo (2023), African governments have generally funded a substantial portion of the continent's infrastructure development on a cash basis, which is restricting infrastructure deployment due to financial constraints. The information was further confirmed by ICA (2018), which stated that, despite perceptions of weak African states dominated by foreign investments, national governments are, in fact, central players in infrastructure delivery, accounting for between 24% and 44% of spending. However, national fiscal and economic challenges constrain African National governments' resources for investment in infrastructural development.

Figure 3.2 confirms the regions where most infrastructural project finance takes place; West Africa has the lion's share, with $16.3 billion, and is followed by East Africa with $13.1 billion. The share of South Africa and Southern Africa is $ 12.4 billion. However, the share of infrastructure development finance in South Africa (5.9 billion dollars) alone is almost equal to that of Southern Africa (6.5 billion dollars) and Central Africa (6.3 billion dollars). Figure 3.2 illustrates that the investment in infrastructure was allocated as follows: transportation, 39.2%; water, 16.9%; energy, 31.9%; ICT, 2.6%; multi-sectoral, 4.4%; and other/unallocated, 5.1%.

Despite this spending by various organisations, both international and African, rural development remains a significant challenge. This challenge could be attributed to a lack of proper planning and national policies for infrastructural development. Figure 3.3 further highlights the major funders for infrastructural development in Africa according to ICA 2019.

The data in Fig. 3.3 further confirm that African countries are the major contributors of finance for infrastructural development, seconded by China. The third-largest sponsor of infrastructural development in Africa is ICA. According to Fig. 3.3, the Infrastructure Consortium for Africa (ICA) members provided $20.2 billion, African countries $37.5 billion, China $25.7 billion, the Private Sector $11.7 billion, and others $5.6 billion. The Infrastructure Consortium for Africa (ICA) comprises members from the G8 (Canada, France, Germany, Italy, Japan, the United Kingdom, the United States, and Russia), the African Development Bank, the World Bank, the European Investment Bank, and the Development Bank of South Africa. Other members include the African Union Commission, the New Partnership for Africa's Development (NEPAD), and Regional Economic

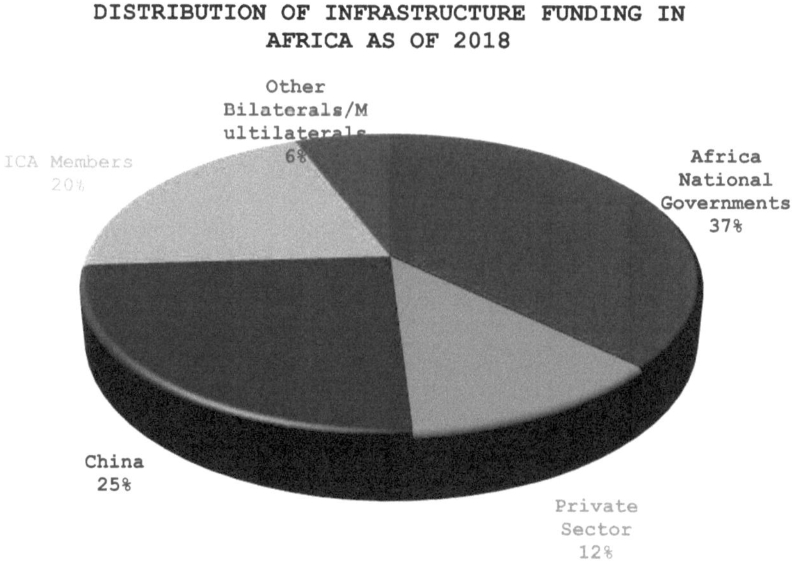

Fig. 3.3 Distribution of infrastructure funding in Africa as of 2018 *Source* ICA 2019

Communities, which act as observers at the ICA meeting. Recently, the G8 has expanded to the G20 by adding several new members, including Argentina, Australia, Brazil, China, the European Union, India, Indonesia, Mexico, Saudi Arabia, South Africa, South Korea, and Turkey. ICA holds meetings where the Consortium determines the direction for regional infrastructure development in Africa. Except for national government funding of infrastructure in Africa, most funds from international organisations and governments are long-term loans that are repayable, as well as grants and aid that must be used for the allocated projects. Many of the financial donors provide expert assistance with infrastructure planning, implementation, supervision, capacity building, financial tools, and support in managing infrastructural programmes and projects. Many international organisations also provide interest rate subsidies that cushion the amount of money that is repayable.

One key finding of this chapter is that Africa faces significant limitations in developing its infrastructure, particularly in rural areas. The main challenges include inadequate road development and transport networks, limited access to electricity, insufficient sanitation facilities, and a shortage of essential goods.

Additionally, the provision of social services, such as education and healthcare, is also lacking. Furthermore, the country's communication networks, including the internet and mobile phone coverage, are underdeveloped networks. Even where mobile networks and the internet are available, connection quality can still be poor due to income disparities and infrastructure gaps in rural areas, which in turn affect rural development. These issues are further complicated by inadequate regulatory systems, limited funding, corruption, inadequate planning, and political interference, all of which hinder the allocation of projects to areas that will have a positive impact. Therefore, it is essential to review existing policies and strategies to ensure that infrastructure developments are implemented sustainably.

4 Examination of Rural Development Policy and Strategy

Abstract

This document examines the policies and strategies for rural development, focusing on boosting the economy and enhancing the quality of life for rural communities. The primary aim is to develop guidelines for improving the economic and social life of rural settlements. The policies and strategies discussed aim to enhance job prospects, reduce poverty, improve access to services, and protect the environment through a holistic and sustainable approach in partnership with key stakeholders. The document explores rural development policies and strategies in Nigeria, Africa, and on an international level, highlighting significant historical and contemporary initiatives. It delves into the colonial and post-independence rural development policies in Nigeria, the African Union's rural development strategies, and international standards shaped by the Sustainable Development Goals (SDGs). The analysis reveals the challenges and successes of various rural development plans, emphasising the need for coordinated efforts, adequate infrastructure, and inclusive approaches to achieve sustainable rural development.

4.1 Introduction

Polices and strategies for rural development naturally focus on boosting the economy and enhancing the quality of life for rural communities. The policy aims to develop guides on improving the economic and social life of rural settlements. Policies and strategies for rural development aim to enhance job prospects, reduce poverty, improve access to services, and protect the environment. To achieve these

C. Osuigwe, *Economic Development of Rural Areas*, Sustainable Development Goals Series, https://doi.org/10.1007/978-3-032-10572-1_4

goals, a holistic and sustainable approach is taken in partnership with key stakeholders. The policies and strategic plans will be examined in Nigeria, Africa, and on an international level.

4.2 Nigeria Rural Development Policy

This section of the chapter discusses two significant areas: the colonial and post-independence rural development of Nigeria.

4.2.1 Colonial Time

British colonial ideology of rural development in Nigeria is categorised into two ideals.

1. The rural areas are seen as primary sources of raw material in the direct exploitation of Nigeria's economy.
2. The rural areas were seen as a primary source of basic agricultural products for food provision to colonial masters and urban dwellers.

The 1902 Planning Ordinance empowered the government to declare certain areas as European Reservations, each with its own Local Board of Health. Moreover, the colonial government's Township Ordinance Act, promulgated in 1917, dictated the developmental course of the rural areas when it classified settlements into first, second, and third classes for infrastructural provision (Badiora, 2020). The Township Ordinance Act of 1917 did not support the development of rural areas. White Europeans and their workers largely foreignised the first-class settlements, and these settlements had a higher concentration of infrastructure; an example is Lagos. The second and third-class settlements were not provided with adequate policy and strategic infrastructural provisions. Abdu and Marshall (1990) described the colonial system as an outlier of Britain's economic space, characterised by an exploitative relationship based on the exportation of agricultural products such as palm oil, cotton, cocoa, and groundnuts. The system supported the use of rural resources in developing cities, and, initially, the First-Class Settlements (White Settlement Areas).

Nigeria's first rural development initiative can be traced back to the Welfare Act of 1945. Iwuagwu (2006) said the Welfare Act had a "Ten Year Plan of Development and Welfare" to develop paths that accelerate colonial exploitation of rural resources. This act led to the establishment of research institutes and marketing boards to improve crop production and control the storage and marketing of crop exports. This act led to the establishment of the Nigerian Cocoa Marketing Board in 1947, and Cotton, Groundnuts, and Oil Palm Boards were established in 1949. These marketing boards were created for the colonial interest of exploiting rural resources. The 1946–1956 development plan was regionalised in 1954 when the Littleton constitution was proclaimed. The colonial rural development plan focused on agricultural productivity, while other important developments were ignored.

Exploiting rural agriculture for economic gain through exports has led to the systematic disempowerment of rural areas in Nigeria, from the pre-independence period to the present day. Since the colonial era, the Nigerian government has faced significant challenges in rural areas due to a lack of basic infrastructure, including sanitation, electricity, piped water, good roads, and healthcare services.

Nevertheless, there were various levels of colonial development, with missionaries participating in rural areas. Missionaries build schools and hospitals in rural areas to support religious activities. They also built skill training centres that taught rural people carpentry, weaving, and pottery in some areas. Raghumani (2012) said that they aimed to spread colonial beliefs. However, they contributed to the growth and development of education in rural areas. Notably, the missionaries' provision of education was not aimed at fostering a political consciousness that would lead to better governance, but rather at creating a tool to safeguard obedience and momentum for the colonial agenda.

4.2.2 Post-Independence Rural Development

The post-independence rural Development of Nigeria was crafted under the following.

1. First National Development Plan (1962–1968).

The plan aimed to foster collaboration between the public and private sectors, as well as between federal and regional governments. The anticipation of superseding the colonial master's exploitation tendencies also drove the first National Development Plan. The plan emphasised agriculture, industry, transport, and manpower development. The foremost priority was to leverage agriculture to develop the rural areas. The endeavour to develop agriculture affects rural areas. However, the plan was an extension of exploiting the rural resources to benefit the urban areas. Abass (1993) explained that the first national development plan witnessed the peasant farmers being forced to produce cash crops for export at the expense of subsistence crops.

The major challenge of the plan was the failure to support rural infrastructural development. Furthermore, its focus was on agricultural produce for export purposes without strengthening the real agricultural base for local and national consumption by providing the necessary infrastructure.

2. National Development Plan (1970–1974).

The second National Development Plan is also known as the Oil Boom Development Plan due to the high earnings generated through the oil sector. It was also during the Nigerian Civil War. Ugwu (2009) stated that at the end of the war, the Second National Development Plan had the following objective:

1. The reconstruction of the damaged facilities and rehabilitation and resettlement of persons displaced by the war.
2. The rehabilitation and resettlement of demobilised armed forces personnel.
3. To establish a resourceful administrative service and an appropriate economic infrastructure, especially in the new states.
4. To bring about a doubling of real income per capita before 1975.

Egonmwan & Ibodje (2001) indicated that a capital expenditure of 3.2 billion naira and an anticipated overall growth rate of 7% per annum were planned. Okoli (2004) explained that the plan developed the Nigerian Enterprises Promotion Decree in 1972, which allowed Nigerian participation in companies with ownership ranging from 40% to 60%; this, however, dispirited foreign investments. The federal government purchased shares in major commercial entities, such as banks and insurance companies. The Second National Development Plan also aimed to reduce inequality among the social classes and between urban and rural areas. The plan's primary focus was not on rural development, as in the First National Development Plan, but on holistic development, where all segments of the Nigerian space and population were to be developed.

Instead of the oil boom during the second national development plan becoming a blessing and a complement to agricultural development, agricultural development was abandoned. The reconstruction, resettlement, and rehabilitation policies were abandoned. The political elites engaged in oil rent, and the spread of corruption started. The decline in the agricultural sector, which had been the mainstay of the economy, led to a growing appetite for food imports. The decline in the agricultural sector also impacted rural agricultural production and development, directly affecting the Nigerian economy.

3. Third National Development Plan (1975–1980).

The Third National Development Plan was also implemented during the oil boom years. The plan's objectives were to distribute income, minimise unemployment, promote economic diversification, and indigenize economic activities. The initial total expenditure for the plan was 30 billion naira (which would be around 30 billion dollars or more at the time).

The plan aimed to curb inflationary tendencies and suggested that the country would achieve a high level of development (Ibetan & Oghator, 2013). The plan was not favourable to rural development like the First National Development Plan. According to Onah (2006) in the Third National Development Plan, "agriculture and social development schemes (education, housing, health, and welfare) that have a direct effect on the livelihood of the rural population (constituting 70% of Nigerian population), had 5% and 11.5% respectively of the financial allocation contained in the plan. The plan was synonymous with the Nigerian budget of 2018, which allocated only 7.04% to education in a country with a high level of illiteracy, particularly in the northern part of Nigeria.

Due to the decline in rural development and high inequality between rural areas and urban areas, the government developed an interest in modernising agriculture through an integrated rural development plan. The government increased budgetary shares to fund diverse and interrelated rural development sectors such as rural agricultural development projects, electrification scheme, nine River Basin Development Authority (RBDAs); the construction of small dams and boreholes for rural water supply; introduction of Operation Feed the Nation and Green Revolution; provided resources to large-scale mechanised state farming enterprises; and public efforts at land reforms through the Land Use Act of 1978. The investments in rural agriculture did not yield the desired results due to inadequate investment in rural infrastructure, such as roads, electricity, and healthcare, among others.

4. Fourth National Development Plan (1985–1990)

The Fourth National Development Plan consolidated the Third National Development Plan, with a greater commitment to industrial development and the oil sector. The plan was to:

1. Development of local investment for export-oriented industries.
2. To add value to locals through the development of small and medium-scale industries.
3. Improve local sourcing of inputs for industrial development.
4. Improving the efficiency of government-owned enterprises.
5. Reduction of unemployment and poverty.
6. Increase the income of Nigerians.
7. Achievement in the development of technological skills among citizens.
8. The generation of electricity will still be a big problem for Nigeria in 2025.

The National Development Plans aimed to significantly improve the standard of living for the average Nigerian. However, the high level of corruption and financial indiscipline led to the failure of the plans and the federal government's debts to institutions. Due to the failure and high debts, the Fourth Development Plan was characterised by huge debt servicing, which weakened its implementation. It was the first plan developed under a democratically elected government and involved the participation of Local Governments. The achievements include commissioning the Egbin Power Station, 87 telephone exchanges throughout Nigeria, the Oku Iboku Newspaper project, Akure Airport, and an increase in educational enrolment at all levels. There were improvements in healthcare services, the construction of thousands of kilometres of federal highways, and the rehabilitation and construction of state roads, as well as the implementation of the Agricultural Development Program (ADP) in seventeen out of the nineteen states of the federation, among others (Onah 2006, and Egonmwan and Ibodje 2001).

The plan emphasised the importance of rural infrastructure development as a means to improve the quality of rural life. It supported an improved budget for the eleven River Basin Development Authorities, whose functions were the construction of boreholes, dams, feeder roads, and jetties. The RBDAs were empowered to develop the rural areas by constructing feeder roads, drilling boreholes and wells, and building farm service centres and earth dams. Because the plan was implemented under a democratic government, there was an increase in plan inclusivity across all tiers and levels of government, leading to enhanced participation in rural development activities and infrastructure provision. According to Filani (1993, p. 250), "the 1981–1985 national development plan marked a turning point in rural development efforts in Nigeria because it was the first to recognise the rural sector as a priority area. It made provisions for integrated packages such as the infrastructure, institutional, and administrative apparatus to facilitate rapid development of the country's agricultural potential".

The significant challenges of the national development plan, from the first to the fourth, include a lack of political will, inadequate feasibility studies and research for proper development, corruption, financial indiscipline, a lack of inclusivity and participation in the development and implementation of the plans, and political and governmental instabilities. However, they cannot dispute that there was progress.

5. The Structural Adjustment Programme and Directorate for Food, Roads, and Rural Infrastructure (1985–1998)

After the Fourth National Development Plan, the Fifth was not implemented separately but was merged into the Structural Adjustment Programme. The programme established the Directorate for Food, Roads, and Rural Infrastructure (DFRRI) in 1985. Its objectives were to provide infrastructure to rural areas and encourage productive activities; to promote socio-cultural and recreational programmes, as well as cohesion activities within and between communities; to enhance communication between citizens and the government; and to support productive sectors such as food and agriculture, rural industrialisation, and technology. DFRRI also sought to make the rural environment more attractive.

Other agencies formed during this period included the National Directorate for Employment (NDE), which supports better life programmes for rural women and dwellers, the People's Bank, and the Directorate of Mass Mobilisation for Social Justice and Economic Recovery (MAMSER).

Overall, during the DFRRI, there was a positive shift towards a more inclusive approach to rural development; although it was not entirely efficient, it proved to be more effective than previous methods. Since the democratic dispensation began in 1999, there are now more inclusive rural development systems. In 1999, a four-year development plan was initiated to create a comprehensive, competitive, and responsive economy that was private sector-led, diversified, market-oriented, and open, yet driven by internal growth (Marcellus, 2009, citing Donli, 2004). However, the private sector did not take the potential of rural development seriously, particularly due to the infrastructural challenges faced by rural areas. The emphasis on private sector-led growth did not convey a clear message for rural development. This affected one of the plan's objectives and hampered the intended action. In 2003, a new plan called the National Economic Empowerment was initiated in response to this challenge.

6. National Economic Empowerment and Development Strategy (NEEDS: 2003–2007).

NEEDS brought together the non-governmental organisation, the private sector, and the public in pursuit of its development goals. By aiming to empower the rural population, NEEDS had a clear vision of eliminating rural poverty and promoting rural development. The focus was on creating youth employment, building rural infrastructure, and managing natural resources. The economic diversity support from NEEDS led to the three levels of government replicating the programme within their spheres. Marcellus (2009) noted that although Nigeria's wealth increased during the NEEDS period, due to improved oil prices and debt relief from the Paris Club, the average Nigerian remained unfairly poor, especially in rural areas.

Other programmes initiated between 1999 and 2025 to support and encourage rural development in Nigeria include the Poverty Alleviation Program (PAP: 1999–2000). The programme was designed to employ approximately 200,000 people, and a sum of NI06 million was set aside for the programme; however, the process was not transparent, and the accountability of the budget was not verified to assess the programme's success. Then, there was the National Poverty Eradication Program (NAPEP), which was designed to direct and monitor the activities of the core poverty eradication departments and Agencies, such as health, education, power and steel, water resources, work, and housing.

Launched in 2011 by the Dr. Goodluck Jonathan government, Youwin aimed to empower Nigerian entrepreneurs by providing grants. This was later followed by the National Social Investment Programme (NSIP), introduced by President Muhammadu Buhari's administration in 2016 as part of its efforts to tackle extreme poverty. The NSIP was designed through N-Power, the National Home-Grown School Feeding Programme, the Government Enterprise and Empowerment Programme (GEEP), and the Conditional Cash Transfer (CCT). These government-sponsored programmes' central focus is to reduce poverty in Nigeria drastically. YouWin was more successful than the NSIP programme and had a well-recorded success.

Examining rural development plans and policies shows a government willingness to enhance rural progress. However, these policies have not achieved the expected outcomes, as rural settlements in Nigeria still face a lack of substantial investment in infrastructure and private sector investment in commerce, agriculture, tourism, and industrial growth. The disparity between the urban and rural areas has led to an exploitative relationship between the two, where urban areas are more favoured than rural areas.

Policy, practice inconsistencies, and corruption have challenged the conceptualisation of rural development since 1995. Most programmes or projects fail due to various factors, including inadequate facilities, poor management, lack of accountability, corruption, and a lack of inclusivity throughout the planning, implementation, and management stages. The politicisation of rural development plans and the absence of professionalism in planning and implementation have conspired to render most rural development efforts difficult, resulting in poor outcomes and limited success.

4.3 African Union Rural Development Policy/Strategies, African Continental Free Trade Area

This subtopic examines the African Union's rural development policies and strategies, including the African Continental Free Trade Area and the New Partnership for Africa's Development (NEPAD). It considers their role in promoting and delivering rural development plans through inclusive methods, as well as in building rural infrastructure, including water, sanitation, roads, and electricity. It also explores how they support economic and social growth through private and public investment and provide essential services such as education and healthcare. Additionally, it addresses the challenges and risks associated with inequality, gender, and youth empowerment, highlighting the need for inclusive approaches.

4.3.1 Africa Rural Development Policy and Strategies

Developing Africa's rural areas has been a challenge since many African countries gained independence. In Sub-Saharan Africa, many countries struggle with infrastructure development. Furthermore, many of the world's poorest nations are also found in Africa, making it challenging to achieve sustainable development in the region's rural areas. Across rural Africa, one cannot help but notice the shortage of basic infrastructure and services, including decent hospitals, education, access roads, water, and sanitation. Additionally, rural areas are characterised by underdeveloped agricultural systems, underperforming commercial systems, and a lack of industrialisation. According to AU (2025), the rural population in Africa stands at 530 million and is projected to surpass 580 million by 2020; about 48 per cent of this population relies directly on agriculture for economic and livelihood survival. Equally, rural African areas are dominated by agricultural production, mainly subsistence farming, with few mechanised farms. Nevertheless, rural populations are expected to continue rising by 2050, making it crucial to address rural population growth through effective rural development plans and stratcgics (AU, 2015).

Plaizier (2016), in his article titled "Truths about Africa's Agriculture", said that there is vast room for improvement, and Africa remains a net food importer. However, it has 60% of the world's uncultivated arable land. Plaizier further highlighted that agricultural production and food security have struggled to keep pace with demand. It is not arguable that Africa has the resources to make the continent food sufficient. The continent also has a hard-working population, but Osuigwe (2024) pointed out that weak leadership is hindering Africa's sustainable development, particularly in rural areas.

The fundamental objective of rural development is to provide sustainable development and quality of life for rural people. AU (2025) states that the expectation of the Africa Agenda 2063 will be a liveable rural community that will come from broad-based breakthroughs in agricultural productivity, investments in education, the building of local institutions, and infrastructure, which allow rural dwellers to be key drivers of agri-based and resource-based value chains that generate high-income levels. Rural settlements will be transformed to enjoy access to sustainable socio-economic indices that will transform their standard of living. Some identified strategies and plans in the African Union Agenda 2063 for Rural development are.

1. Rural communities should be equipped with current communication, education, sanitation, and health facilities and should have vibrant, dynamic market economies. Rural dwellers should have access to affordable and decent housing, including housing finance, all the necessities of life, and social capital that improves livelihood standards.
2. There should be a reduction in income disparities between rural dwellers and urban households, leading to more inclusive and cohesive communities. This could be achieved by enhancing the human resources and potential of rural areas.
3. Rural communities will be connected to the rest of the economy through roads, energy, mobile communication networks, water, sanitation, and hygiene systems.
4. Rural areas of Africa in 2063 should be key drivers of agri-based and resource-based value chains that generate high-income levels. Rural dwellers should have access to social services and infrastructure comparable to those in urban areas.

5. Over 95 per cent of rural women should enjoy access to productive wealth, including land, credit, inputs, and financial and insurance services.
6. Countries should put in place proper strategies to address the following features

(i) Prevalence of rural poverty; and
(ii) Feminisation of poverty.

7. At the continental level, the African Union has adopted the Social Policy Framework (SPF), which encourages Member States to extend coverage and provide a minimum package of services to the poor and vulnerable. Social protection plans target the informal economy and rural workers since most of the labour force is engaged in the informal economy and rural sector, with low social security coverage.
8. African countries should develop social protection and minimum packages to advance access to critical healthcare and basic income security for children and families, women and men of working age, in the informal economy and rural sector, as well as older persons.

The achievement of the Agenda 2063 Goals is at the centre of sustainable development in Africa and the reform of the African Union Commission. Sustainable Rural Development is vital to a nation's economic, social, and environmental viability. The manifestation of poverty goes beyond the urban-rural divide and has sub-regional and regional contexts. It is, therefore, critical and of great value to coordinate rural development initiatives that contribute to sustainable livelihoods through global, regional, national, and local efforts, as appropriate.

4.3.2 African Continental Free Trade Area (AFCFTA)

The AFCFTA's primary objective is to enhance trade among African countries, increase Africa's competitiveness on the global stage, raise Africa's real income to 7% by 2035, and reduce the number of people living in extreme poverty. ElGanainy et al. (2023) noted that AFCFTA should not only be a trade pact but a strategy to transform economic landscapes, improve political stability, and foster equitable and sustainable development. Therefore, AFCFTA should be capable of transforming rural development through trade and services, as most of the African population resides in rural areas; otherwise, the ideology will fail. A sustainable framework for trade should positively impact market accessibility for agricultural goods, foster a reinforced inflow of foreign investments, and facilitate the possibility of rural industrialisation (Douwe et al., 2017). Furthermore, the success of the AFCFTA in improving rural economies in Africa will depend on countries' policies and strategies for infrastructural development and other services linked to the AFCFTA. There is substantial evidence of a lack of infrastructure in various African nations, a significant obstacle to commerce (Kaiser & Barstow, 2022). However, the proper strategy could minimise the effects. Nonetheless, the AFCFTA Agreement demonstrates the potential for significant social and economic integration to support sustainable rural development. Nevertheless, it is important to address the issues of rural infrastructural development and regional economic development corridors that will integrate and connect rural social and economic activities to market opportunities and job opportunities.

The AFCFTA plans do not have a direct impact or a specific plan for revolutionising rural development. However, it is essential to address the issues that limit the linkages between rural potentials and opportunities to benefit from the AFCFTA. The AFCFTA plan can significantly enhance market opportunities and development for rural settlements in Africa. As a result, different African countries need to plan how to connect their transport networks, energy supplies, and communication systems, which are essential for linking rural producers to local, regional, and global markets.

4.3.3 New Partnership for Africa's Development (NEPAD)

Launched by the African Union, the New Partnership for Africa's Development (NEPAD) was established to tackle social and economic challenges and boost rural development. NEPAD aims to address the challenges faced by rural residents through job creation, entrepreneurship promotion, and income growth, as many Africans reside in rural areas with limited social and economic opportunities. NEPAD's objectives are to foster sustainable social and economic growth, reduce poverty, integrate the African economy into the global economy, and empower women. According to NEPAD (….), the strategic direction of NEPAD is divided into six themes:

1. Agriculture and Food Security
2. Climate Change and Natural Resource Management
3. Regional Integration and Infrastructure

4. Human Development
5. Economic and Corporate Governance
6. Cross-Cutting Issues—Gender, ICT, Capacity Development, and Communication

To address the above, NEPAD has the following rural development programmes and projects: NEPAD (….)

1. Comprehensive Africa Agriculture Development Programme (CAADP)

A. NEPAD Food and Nutrition Security Programme—This programme aims to reduce hunger through research, capacitating policymakers and strategic specialists across various sectors, and supporting the implementation of practical solutions.
B. NEPAD Pan-Africa Cassava Initiative (NPACI)—supporting cassava initiatives to reduce hunger, increase income, and create opportunities in rural areas.
C. African Fertiliser Financing Mechanism (AFFM)—to enable the production, distribution, procurement, and use of fertiliser in Africa to help develop rural areas and create more opportunities and empowerment.
D. African Biosciences Initiative (ABI)—Harnessing biological applications for improved agriculture productivity over five years.
E. Partnership for African Fisheries (PAF)—Boosting Africa's Most Valuable Renewable Natural Assets—Fishing.
F. TerrAfrica Programme—Leveraging funds to scale up sustainable land organisation in sub-Saharan Africa.
G. The Rural Futures Programme—To place prominence on the agriculture sector stratagems to accelerate social and economic change in rural Africa

According to NEPAD (….), since its endorsement in 2003, thirty-four African countries have signed up to the CAADP, and eight have surpassed the 10% target, including Burkina Faso, Ethiopia, Ghana, Guinea, Malawi, Mali, Niger, and Senegal. This programme has motivated many African countries to allocate more resources to agricultural development, particularly in rural areas, and make substantial progress towards increasing food production, providing access to nutritious food, and reducing poverty.

2. Programme for Infrastructure Development in Africa (PIDA)

A. Transport—Cutting transport costs—The ideology links the continent's primary production and consumption centres and major cities and opens land-locked countries. This project could contribute to rural development and the integration of African rural areas into the regional market chain by establishing properly planned road networks.
B. Energy—Empowering Africans with Energy—If properly planned and implemented, it could help electrify rural communities and open more opportunities for rural industrialisation, entrepreneurship, and economic production.
C. Information and Communication Technology—Access to mobile phones and the cost of data could be reduced through this process, particularly in rural areas; it could lead to increased access to marketing rural communities' products and higher investments.
D. Water—Ensuring Water Security—Nine transboundary water projects aimed to develop multipurpose dams and increase the capacity for water transfers within the River Basin region that rural development could leverage to improve rural economic production.

3. Education and Training

   NEPAD is improving frontline healthcare in Africa by mobilising funds from bilateral partners to support training nurses and midwives and enhance African-led healthcare research. This will improve the health conditions in rural areas and directly enhance productivity. There is a relationship between health and productivity.

4. Gender

NEPAD's Gender Programme unlocks the unexploited potential of African women living in rural areas with minimal income. The key areas of intervention are business skills advancement, vocational training, access to microfinance, support to women SMMEs, women in cross-border trade and creation of business incubators; gender mainstreaming in local governance; prevention and rehabilitation of women victims of gender-based violence, agriculture, food security and nutrition, advocacy for women's human rights and gender justice, as well as information technology.

5. Capacity Development

NEPAD developed a policy guide on capacity development, known as the Capacity Development Strategic Framework (CDSF). CDSF aims to accomplish integrated capacity results at all levels to create a results-oriented and people-driven development path. Key priorities for the CDSF are enhancing human, institutional, and knowledge-based capacity, creating enabling environments, and changing mindsets.

Despite the African Union's well-designed policies and strategic plans, which can directly and indirectly support rural development, poverty remains a persistent issue in Africa's rural areas. The ongoing struggle against rural poverty and underdevelopment may be due to the lack of coordinated policy development between regional bodies and national governments. Furthermore, the underdevelopment of rural areas in Africa could be attributed to the shortage of experts available to support the initiation, planning, implementation, monitoring, and evaluation of rural development projects. Other factors contributing to this issue may include limited community involvement, inadequate funding, which can lead to project delays, and potentially high levels of corruption due to inadequate accountability and transparency.

4.4 International Standards on Rural Development

The following strategies and ideologies shape the history of rural development worldwide.

1. The 1950s to 1960s were the era of modernisation approaches emphasising technology transfer.
2. The 1970s were an era of government intervention and integrated rural development programmes.
3. The 1980s are associated with market liberalisation and attempts to roll back the state.
4. The 1990s marked an era of community participation and empowerment within the framework of diversifying rural livelihood options.
5. 2000s till the present is focused on the goals of the Millennium Development Goals and the United Nations Sustainable Development Goals, particularly in the areas of poverty eradication, support to agriculture, security of tenure, innovations, sustainable farming systems, and the location of producers within global value chains

This book explores the effect of the United Nations' Sustainable Development Goals (SDGs) on rural development. The SDGs seek to promote rural development by providing strategies and plans for public and private institutions, as well as NGOs, to establish a framework that fosters sustainable social and economic growth while safeguarding the environment. Key strategies for rural development under the SDGs include access to quality education, poverty alleviation, infrastructure development to connect rural areas with markets, services, and technologies, and access to modern energy services that enhance productivity and health. Other strategies include conservation, organic farming, and afforestation to maintain ecological balance, as well as supporting rural-urban linkages, collaborative efforts, and equitable resource distribution to drive social and economic development. The SDGS that contribute to rural development are.

A. **SDG 1**- No poverty: Every other SDG is linked to SDG 1, as they all focus on eliminating poverty and achieving a decent standard of living for everyone, regardless of whether they live in urban or rural areas. Poverty has been a persistent issue for centuries, perpetuating cycles of inequality and social and economic exclusion, which stop individuals and communities from reaching their full potential. World Bank (2021) states that more than 700 million people worldwide still live in extreme poverty, struggling to meet their basic needs for food, shelter, and healthcare. Then, SDG 1 offers a framework to mobilise resources, encourage partnerships, and provide tools to alleviate poverty. SDG 1 encourages stakeholders, including private and public organisations, to create sustainable and inclusive development pathways in rural and urban areas. The success of SDG 1 will be a greater achievement for the broader SDGs from 2 to 17. Rural development and poverty alleviation strategies should include the development of infrastructure that is accessible to both domestic and international markets, access to ensure resource development and utilisation, access to basic services and social protection systems, and support for robust agricultural practices that boost food security and increase household income.
B. **SDG 2-** Zero Hunger: Addressing rural development is a major milestone for SDG 2, which aims to eradicate hunger by ensuring access to nutritious, safe, and sufficient food. To accomplish this, farming practices need to be advanced, farmers' incomes must increase, and access to land ownership and labour conditions should be improved. SDG 2 comprises eight goals: ending hunger, achieving food security, improving nutrition, and promoting sustainable agriculture. The primary focus of SDG 2 covers various forms of farming, including livestock farming, fisheries, cultivation, pastoralism, and aquaculture.
C. **SDG 4** - Quality Education: The United Nations (2019) reported that discrepancies between rural and urban areas are evident, and approximately 85

per cent of countries (with available data) reported higher out-of-school rates for primary and secondary schools in rural areas compared to urban areas. According to the United Nations (2017, p. 13), SDG4 should be "inclusion and equity: All people, irrespective of sex, age, race, colour, ethnicity, language, religion, political or another opinion, national or social origin, property or birth, as well as persons with disabilities, migrants, indigenous peoples, and children and youth, especially those in vulnerable situations or other status, should have access to inclusive, equitable quality education and lifelong learning opportunities". SDG 4 supports the idea of educating Vulnerable groups, including the poor, disabled, Indigenous peoples, and ethnic minorities. For a successful SDG 4 in rural development, strategies and policies should also support gender equality in education.

SDG 4 aims to ensure that all youths and children have access to free and quality primary and secondary education, support early childhood care through pre-primary education, and encourage the development of acceptable literacy and numeracy skills. Other SDG4 targets include access to relevant skills in the workplace, supporting safe and inclusive education environments, and ensuring that teachers and educators receive quality training and better working conditions.

D. **SDG 6**- "90 per cent of people live in rural areas, and the majority live in just two regions with 558 million in Central Asia and Southern Asia and 220 million in sub-Saharan Africa" (United Nations, 2018, p. 12). WHO (2014) further estimated that, in the next reporting cycle, only one-third of the 94 countries surveyed had complete human resource strategies for both urban and rural areas related to drinking water, sanitation, and hygiene. "Some 159 million people in 2015 still collect drinking water from distant surface water sources, mostly rural communities in Central and Southern Asia and Sub-Saharan Africa" (United Nations 2018, p139). SDG 6 is an area where rural development plays a crucial role—many have access to safe and affordable drinking water and suitable sanitation facilities. SDG 6 supports rural development through investments in sanitation and water infrastructure, the protection of water-related ecosystems, the education of rural populations on water efficiency and hygiene, and the support of communities in water and sanitation management.
E. **SDG 11** - Sustainable cities and communities: Finally, SDG 11 aims to make rural settlements and cities safe, resilient, and sustainable. It supports integrated and inclusive planning and community participation for sustainable human settlements. SDG 11 supports sustainable territorial planning,

and it is crucial to promote rural development, ensuring access to basic services, enhancing connectivity and mobility, and preserving cultural and natural heritage. Furthermore, the goal of SDG 11 is to promote positive social, economic, and environmental relationships between urban, peri-urban, and rural areas. It is achievable by reinforcing national, regional, and local development of sustainable territorial planning. Therefore, governments at all levels should espouse integrated territorial planning that supports inclusive efficiency, resource efficiency, and adaptation to climate change.

Considering the examination of the 5 SDGs that directly impact the sustainability of rural planning and development mentioned above, it's also worth noting that rural development has a ripple effect on nearly all the SDGs, both directly and indirectly. For instance, SDG 5 focuses on gender equality, with notably high levels of inequality often found in rural areas. Therefore, incorporating SDG 5 into gender policy during programme and project initiation, planning, and implementation can help reduce these inequalities. Similarly, SDG 3 (Good Health and Well-being) can address health issues in rural areas, including mortality rates, promote healthy living, improve child health, and combat communicable diseases. It will help improve accessibility to health facilities in rural areas. Furthermore, poverty and health are interrelated, and rural development can contribute to achieving SDG3 by reducing poverty. SDG 10 (Reduced Inequalities) supports rural development through inclusive investment in agribusiness, small industrial investments, and tourism development in rural areas, increasing income in rural areas and reducing inequality between urban and rural settlements. SDG 10 addresses technology disparities between urban and rural areas by supporting the improvement of communication infrastructure and connectivity, thereby reducing high inequality in rural areas.

For rural development to succeed, it needs to take an integrated approach that considers the social, economic, and environmental aspects of the Sustainable Development Goals (SDGs). Rural development policies and strategies should align with the SDGs to encourage links between rural and urban areas, promote collaborative efforts, invest in infrastructure, and provide rural areas with access to markets, technology, and education that support sustainable economic growth. Furthermore, supporting policies and strategies that enhance innovation, private and public investment, and private-public partnerships in rural development investments. The SDGs will help address the exceptional challenges that rural areas face; by addressing these challenges, Africa can make significant strides towards more sustainable rural development.

Rural Development Case Studies 5

Abstract

This chapter reviews case studies as qualitative evidence of social and economic growth. Three international case studies are examined: from a developed, Transitional, and Developing Country, and two from Africa. The goal is to show that effective rural development can sustainably improve rural lives and encourage urban-to-rural migration. International case studies include Zhejiang Rural Development in China, illustrating land circulation fostering agricultural, industrial growth, and migration; Boekel, Netherlands, re-using farm buildings for commercial purposes; and Petrolina-Juazeiro in Brazil, with irrigation projects transforming the economy and reducing rural poverty. African case studies include Nigeria's community-led Development project in Ahiazu Mbaise and South Africa's Rural Development Programme and Youth Service Corps, aimed at economic growth and sustainable communities.

5.1 Introduction

The book examines the concepts and realities of rural development, highlighting both the challenges and opportunities, as well as its weaknesses and strengths. It is significant for this book to review some rural development case studies. These will serve as qualitative data that emphasise first-hand information on rural social and economic development and growth. It examines the patterns that influence migration from rural-to-urban areas and vice versa. This chapter analyses three international case studies (one from a Developed Country, one from a Transitional Country, and one from a Developing Country) along with two African case studies. The aim is to find evidence that if rural development is planned and

C. Osuigwe, *Economic Development of Rural Areas*, Sustainable Development Goals Series, https://doi.org/10.1007/978-3-032-10572-1_5

executed successfully, it will sustainably enhance the lives of rural populations and stimulate urban-to-rural migration.

5.2 International Case Study

The international case study examines a transitional country, using the Zhejiang land circulation programme as a key example. It also investigates developed countries, drawing on a case study of "Moutheoeve Re-using Vacant Farm Buildings in Boekel, the Netherlands", for commercial purposes. Furthermore, it considers developing countries, citing Petrolina-Juazeiro (Brazil) as an example of integrated rural development. These case studies are described below.

5.2.1 Transitional Country: Zhejiang Rural Development (Land Circulation Programme) in China

The land policy in China emphasises public ownership over private ownership because of the socialist government system. In 1978, China introduced reforms that resulted in extensive rural-to-urban migration and swift urbanisation. However, despite public land ownership, farmers retain the right to use the land for a period of 30 years. The Chinese land tenure system did not allow for agriculture and bigger farms to be commercialised. There were limitations to agricultural activities and production. The limitations and challenges of the Chinese land tenure system led to the introduction of land circulation and moderate-scale operations in 2014.

According to Tong and Lo (2021), land circulation refers to the transfer of land use rights to other farmers or economic organisations with contracted land management rights. Through the Land Circulation Framework, the Zhejiang provincial government guided organisations and individuals within its jurisdiction to participate in land circulation, allowing land contracts and management rights to be transferred to family farms and agricultural cooperative organisations run by villagers, thereby facilitating the large-scale operation of rural land (Tong & Lo, 2021). The provincial government also reinvigorated land circulation in manufacturing and commercial activities. This allowed for large-scale agricultural activities and production. Tao and Xu (2007) noted that the transformation of agricultural land and rural construction land alters the spatial development of rural areas, promoting the construction of factories, urban housing, and infrastructure. This programme led to massive farming and industrial growth, creating many jobs and triggering rural-to-urban migration.

According to Tong and Lo (2021), since 2003, Zhejiang Province has implemented various rural development programmes, including the Thousand Villages Demonstration (2003), the Ten Thousand Villages Renovation project (2003), the Beautiful Village policy (2010), the Characteristic Towns policy (2016), and Rural Revitalisation (2018). These programmes have driven the transformation of rural industries, rural facilities, and ecological sustainability. In 2018, the Chinese government emphasised that talent and skill are the key to rural revitalisation. The rural revitalisation led to pilot project areas where talented and skilled people returned to their rural areas to develop small manufacturing and agricultural activities. Zhejiang Province was also designated as one of the national pilot areas due to its successes in implementing rural development plans. It promoted many urban dwellers returning to their rural areas to state business and other forms of production.

Zhejiang Province's rural development programme provides evidence that rural areas' industrial development can offer more jobs, business, and production opportunities, which will attract migrants and returnees. This case study is significant for rural development policymakers and strategic developers who aim to increase rural in-migration and rural return migration to grasp rural revitalisation and decrease the gap between urban and rural areas. The rural economy of Zhejiang province is stimulated by encouraging land circulation to support the land use of new industries in rural areas. The land circulation policy also led to the development of an industrial chain and increased market value, alongside other social and economic activities.

5.2.2 Developed Country: Re-Using Vacant Farm Buildings for Commercial Purposes: A Case from the Moutheoeve in Boekel at Netherlands

Moutheoeve is located in the municipality of Boekel, Netherlands. It is a former dairy farm and has been redeveloped into a commercial shopping centre. Boekel is an area with many landless pig farms. Over the last few decades, numerous policy initiatives have been implemented to reduce the concentration of pig farms due to their environmental impact (Janssen-Jansen, 2008). Koreman and Altes (2023) state that the municipality bought the farm in 2007. In 2015, a local entrepreneur acquired the farm from the municipality and developed a plan to reuse it for catering services and a mall featuring craft shops. The entrepreneur's idea and strategy were to contribute to rural development and create new ideas and jobs. The mall and enterprising area host 20 companies, including a craft nut shop, a flower shop, a hairdresser, a yoga studio, and a home furnisher (Koreman & Altes, 2023). The developments taking place at Mouthoeve serve as a prime example of Boekel's governance approach. The redevelopment of Mouthoeve from a pig farm to a commercial mall has made Boekel an appealing municipality. The municipality's adaptability appears to support the success of Mouthoeve.

The Mouthoeve Mall project has made a positive contribution to the rural community, despite initial reservations expressed by some residents. The community appreciates the enhanced value that has increased their chances of buying locally. Furthermore, Mouthoeve entices young and female entrepreneurs who would have been elsewhere or not have started a business (Koreman & Altes, 2023).

One of the advantages of the rural project is that it is a private initiative with the support of the local municipality, which has relaxed its regulatory policy. It also appeals to entrepreneurs because of its smaller shops, low rents, and flexible lease contracts. Some shop owners had searched across the broader region for business opportunities and ultimately opted for Mouthoeve (Koreman & Altes, 2023). The project opens opportunities, and the businesses operating in the mall offer jobs to employees from the rural community. Therefore, the practice directly contributes to regeneration in Boekel. Mouthoeve exemplifies how a former farm building can be a suitable venue to revitalise rural development, particularly near a town. The presence of a determined local entrepreneur and a flexible governance approach are additional crucial factors. However, this flexibility carries the risk of potential disparities in treatment compared to other entrepreneurs.

5.2.3 Developing Country: Petrolina-Juazeiro (Brazil)

The Petrolina-Juazeiro region is located in the São Francisco River Basin in Northeastern Brazil. In the 1960s and 1970s, this region was among the poorest in Brazil. Its economy was primarily based on traditional agricultural systems, focusing on cotton, livestock, maize, and beans. Following government intervention in the mid-1990s to introduce irrigation in the Petrolina-Juazeiro area, rural poverty decreased as high-value crops, such as mangoes and table grapes—primarily for export—and a variety of other crops, mainly for the local consumption market, were cultivated. "By 2005, the total exports of grapes and mango from

Petrolina-Juazeiro reached close to USD 110 million, representing around 40 per cent of the total exports of fruits from Brazil" (Damiani, 2008, p.5). Since the government's irrigation project at Petrolina-Juazeiro, the area accounts for 98 per cent of Brazil's grape exports and 92 per cent of mango exports. Furthermore, the high production has increased the demand for both skilled and unskilled labour. The significant increase in production led to improved job creation and enhanced the wages and living conditions of rural Petrolina-Juazerio. The successful rural development of Petrolina-Juazerio, driven by irrigation projects and high productivity, has attracted migrants from both rural and urban areas in Northeast Brazil. It also encouraged rural-urban migration and reduced migration of rural people to urban areas.

Before the success of Petrolina-Juazerio, more than 70 per cent of the adult population was illiterate, and this dramatically changed in the 1990s due to heavy investments in irrigation infrastructure carried out by federal government agencies (Damiani, 2008). The irrigation promoted economic and social changes, leading to investment in other economic activities. The economic and social transformation of Petrolina-Juazeiro was largely due to the Brazilian government's involvement in creating agencies to promote the development of the São Francisco River Basin, such as the São Francisco Valley Superintendence and the São Francisco Valley Development Agency.

The Petrolina-Juazeiro irrigation scheme divided the land into plots and built on-farm irrigation infrastructure. The area has social and economic facilities, including schools, health centres, and housing. The completed work is let out to producers, and the operation (water distribution and collection of water fees) and maintenance of the projects are carried out. By 2006, Companhia de Desenvolvimento dos Vales do São Francisco e do Parnaíba (CODEVASF) had constructed six irrigation projects in Petrolina-Juazeiro, covering nearly 46,000 hectares of irrigated land, comprising over 200 agricultural firms, around 2200 small farmers, and more than 100 agricultural specialists (Damiani, 2008). Growers out of the government-sponsored irrigation projects had developed an additional area of 77,000 hectares of irrigated lands, making a total of 120,000 hectares with irrigation; approximately 40,000 workers were employed, which was 30% of the rural labour force in the region, and the region had reached more than 100,000 wage workers (Damiani, 2008). Brazil's government intervention that led to the success of Petrolina-Juazeiro can be summarised as follows:

1. Irrigation of land for agricultural purposes.
2. Planting of crops that are designated for export, such as mangoes and grapes.
3. Investment in agricultural research in the area.

4. Provision of small credit to small farmers.
5. Helping to market and attract firms to invest in the area and assisting in creating a value chain for farmers.
6. Provision of land to farmers in government sponsored irrigation projects.
7. Liaising and supporting the transfer of technology from firms to small farmers, and this process is overseen by the Bank of Northeast Brazil, which provides both credit and professional help in technology transfer between agricultural firms and small farmers.
8. Strengthening rural farmers' unions and assisting in mediation and stakeholders' engagement where necessary.

5.3 Africa Case Study

The African case studies explore different development pathways, including rural development through community-led projects, which are more common in eastern Nigeria, and an integrated rural development approach in South Africa. The two case studies are detailed below.

5.3.1 Communities Self Rural Development Project: Ahiazu Mbaise, Imo State, Nigeria

This subsection of the book is based on my 40 years of personal observation in the area and 20 years of active involvement in community and rural development in the Ahiazu Mbaise Local Government Area. The local government is in a rural area with many rural communities. The rural local government has a population of 237,400 with a density of 2384, while the total area is 99.59 square kilometres. The local government has five social and economic rural nodes: AforOru/Ahiara, AforOgbe, NkwoAla, OfoUkwu/Amabarnax, and AfoUzi. These rural nodes are located along major roads of Owerri Mbaise Road and Mbaise Okpula Road.

In the early 1980s, the governor of Imo State (Sam Mbakwe) carried out some of the best rural infrastructural development in Nigeria. He built the Amaraku Power Station, which provided electricity to many rural communities. However, in some places, he was unable to step down the high-tension electrification to lower tension, thereby enabling proper accessibility to the rural population. Many rural communities rely on self-help through community contributions to generate electricity, thereby accessing energy for commercial, agricultural, and domestic uses. Sam Mbakwe constructed many rural roads that linked rural communities to major towns, including Aba, Owerri, Umuahia, and Okigwe, as well as sources of economic opportunities. He also built a water supply and sanitation.

The construction of this infrastructure in the 1980s was leveraged to transform the rural communities and commercial nodes in the rural local government of Ahiazu Mbaise. The infrastructure provision in the local government led to small-scale farming and agricultural production, as well as small-scale industrial activities, improvements in commercial activities such as retail shops and entertainment centres, and services. Among the five nodes, the biggest node is the AforOru/Ahiara Node, seconded by the OfoOgbe Node, then NkwoAla Node, and then the AforUkwu/Amabarnax Node. For instance, the AforOru/Ahiara node has evolved from a rural node to a pre-urban node, characterised by various forms of urban activities. What helped the transformation was the accessibility to mobile phones, the Internet, and mobile Internet in 2005. The AforOru/Ahiara node has branches of all the major banks in Nigeria, including Zenith Bank, Access Bank, First Bank, Ecobank, and United Bank for Africa. It is a hub of commercial activities, with light industries such as bottled water production, toilet paper production, and bread production, among others. The rural node of AforOru/Ahaira is booming with other services, including electrical parts markets, building materials markets, supermarkets, petrol stations, car repair and service centres. Numerous commercial activities are taking place in the nodes. The banks provide easy banking and transactions for entrepreneurs, although there is still limited access to credit through these commercial banks.

Most of these businesses started with self-help. Ahaizu Mbaise has experienced tremendous transformation. Four-star hotels are in the area, and high-end restaurants serve a variety of local and international cuisine. The node is gradually developing in terms of residential accommodations. Sustainable agriculture, which used to be the mainstay of the local government, is diminishing because of high-level commercial activities, and the youths are no longer interested in subsistence farming. However, some youths engage in poultry and fish farming, which they supply to hotels and restaurants in the local government and big towns that are 50 to 100 kilometres away, such as Umuahia, Aba, Okigwe, and Owerri, the state's capital. However, more is needed as more graduates and skilled people enter the area.

Some graduates are returning to the local government, while others are opting not to move to big cities because they can achieve their dreams in their rural communities within the Ahaizu Local Government. Most houses and new buildings are constructed by local engineers who graduated from higher institutions. The building materials are easily accessed from the regional building and construction market in the AforOru/Ahiara Node.

The major challenge for nodes and rural settlements is the lack of social facilities, such as quality hospitals and schools. The area also required a higher institution to train these rural dwellers in managing and growing their businesses, enabling them to compete with other chain stores and formal businesses. Another challenge is access to credit facilities; most entrepreneurs and those who wish to start their businesses are unable to do so because they lack access to credit. Although banks are located within the local government, there are no government grants or credit systems in place to assist and empower rural entrepreneurs who wish to start their businesses. Where there is access to credit facilities from commercial private banks, the interest rate is so high that rural businesses cannot afford to take up the credit. It is impossible for a youth who wants to start a business to borrow at an interest rate of over 25 per cent. Additionally, some of the roads constructed by Sam Mbakwe require reconstruction due to their extremely poor condition.

The examination of the AforOru/Ahaira rural node reveals the resilience of rural people in developing themselves with little to no help from the government. It highlights that if the government can provide basic infrastructure, such as water, electricity, good roads, and sanitation, to rural areas in Nigeria, many rural communities will live a comfortable life, jobs will be created, productivity will increase, and there will be minimal migration from rural-to-urban areas. It also shows that rural communities can mobilise to empower themselves to provide their own infrastructure, such as electricity and water, that allows them to participate in social and economic activities. These nodes in the local government have often replaced their transformer after waiting for months, but the government has failed to replace them.

The government can leverage existing community stakeholders' systems to implement successful rural development programmes. According to Nekwaya (2007), community participation is the anchor of rural development programmes. Robust community participation in rural development will lead to healthy and sustainable development, but it requires an enabling policy and strategy. The World Bank (2004) asserts that the present era is characterised by efforts to promote citizens' participation in community development, which necessitates a fundamental shift in attitudes and approaches by encouraging planning at the grassroots level with the communities.

5.3.2 South Africa Comprehensive Rural Development Programme and National Rural Youth Service Corps

In 2010, the South African government's Department of Rural Development and Land Reform established a Comprehensive Rural Development Programme (CRDP) to develop rural areas. The CRDP aims to make rural areas vibrant and sustainable rural communities. The ideology also transforms rural youth into job seekers and entrepreneurs. This initiative aims to reduce unemployment in rural areas, create jobs, alleviate poverty, and promote the development of rural communities into sustainable social and economic entities.

Furthermore, in September 2010, the National Rural Youth Service Corps (NARYSEC) was established to employ unemployed rural youth, provide training in technical and vocational skills, promote civic education and instil discipline and nationalism, support their entrepreneurial development, facilitate access to employment, and encourage participation in community service projects. NARYSEC is a programme that targets youths between the ages of 18 and 35 who must be South African citizens. According to DRDLR (2014), the objectives of the NARYSEC programme are.

1. To develop a cadre of young people at the cutting edge of rural development.
2. To develop the character and self-worth of the young people.
3. To organise and empower rural youth to become agents of change and development. Communities can participate in implementing the CRDP.
4. To create a major countryside revolution for socio-economic freedom through nation-building and community service.
5. To promote a result-oriented national rural youth service and build patriotism and social cohesion.

The programme started with pilot projects and infrastructure initiatives in 83 wards across South Africa, mainly targeting 23 prioritised district municipalities. These pilots involve creating food gardens and providing training in gardening, financial management, and community-based planning. The NARYSEC skills training covers areas such as construction, animal and veldt management, farm ranging, record keeping, and disaster management. According to Sizani (2012), the following projects have been initiated with progress made.

1. 44 communities were involved in conservation agriculture technologies, to make more sustainable use of natural resources and improve food production.

2. Indigenous Knowledge Systems (IKS) was another area being developed and a focus of research.
3. The Department had created 11,400 jobs linked to skills development and 3936 in Infrastructure Development. The total number of jobs thus created was 15,336, including NARYSEC.
4. 3258 food gardens had been established, and 190,713 households were profiled, including those for the War on Poverty. 3819 people had been trained in master gardening, household food gardening, financial management, community-based planning, participatory rural appraisal and household profiling, arts and crafts, and Indigenous seed production.
5. Approximately 658 cooperatives and stakeholder councils have been established.
6. Since the inception of the NARYSEC programme, approximately 600 youths have graduated from various Further Education and Training (FET) Colleges in the Western Cape. 500 youths reported for training at De Brug near Bloemfontein on 30 January 2011.
7. Regarding Rural Disaster Mitigation Services (RDMS), three projects were implemented: training vulnerable communities, social relief, and establishing disaster management help desks. Over 500 jobs were created for social relief, and 30 jobs were created for community training.

The programme's challenge involved coordinating between national and provincial sector departments to achieve integrated delivery and reporting, while also ensuring successful graduation from Phases 1 and 2 of the CRDP model. Additionally, there were issues related to the institutional capacity of communities to lead development and governance efforts. These challenges affected certain areas, where stakeholders struggled to participate transparently in implementing interventions.

5.4 Summary

The rural development case studies have explored how various initiatives improve quality of life and boost social and economic well-being in rural areas. Each of the five case studies has a different focus; the first examines land tenure initiatives aimed at developing commercial farming systems that increase productivity and decrease urban-to-rural migration. The second demonstrates how leveraging existing potential can advance rural development and promote entrepreneurship. The third highlights government efforts to provide financial and infrastructural support, leading to higher production and wages. The fourth showcases community dedication to rural development, even with limited government assistance, through infrastructure projects like roads, electricity, and internet access. The fifth emphasises the national government's role in launching a rural development program to empower youth.

These case studies demonstrate that rural development can be achieved through various methods; however, successful implementation depends heavily on effective communication and the active involvement and participation of residents. They emphasise the importance of infrastructure, healthcare, training, education, irrigation, financial credit, agricultural initiatives, community participation, income diversification, sustainable farming, and capacity building as key factors to foster social and economic progress in rural areas.

The case studies highlighted that projects should be prioritised by tailoring interventions to meet specific needs and challenges. They underscore the importance of leveraging local culture and natural beauty to expand rural incomes, thereby creating income and employment opportunities for rural communities. The studies also assessed the long-term sustainability of interventions beyond initial implementation, discussing both positive and negative impacts on rural life. Additionally, the book advocates for integrated, inclusive rural development programmes that consider land tenure systems, social and economic infrastructure, access to finance, indigenous systems, and ways to overcome rural bottlenecks. These efforts aim to promote commercial activities, agriculture, farming, tourism, environmental sustainability, and cultural heritage. It also emphasises targeted projects such as Zhejiang's land reform and the Petrolina-Juazerio irrigation system to support export-oriented farming.

Rural Development Challenges in Africa

6

Abstract

This chapter explores the challenges in African rural development, focusing on issues like limited infrastructure—such as roads, electricity, water, sanitation, and internet access—which restricts service availability, slows economic growth, and increases inequalities. It points out that weak education and healthcare facilities hinder human capital development and reduce quality of life. The chapter stresses the need to promote rural goods and services to improve access for producers. Additionally, it addresses the difficulties faced by rural businesses and entrepreneurs, including poor transportation and communication networks. The text discusses climate change's impact on rural development, especially in agriculture, highlighting how unpredictable weather like droughts and floods threatens food security, income, and infrastructure. It explains that land tenure security promotes investment and productivity, while insecurity hampers progress. The challenges of financial exclusion in rural areas are examined, showing that limited access to finance affects investment, productivity, and poverty. Weak governance—marked by low political will, accountability, transparency issues, corruption, and limited community involvement—is identified as a significant barrier. Environmental degradation, including deforestation, overgrazing, and harmful farming practices, is also addressed. The chapter concludes that sustainable rural development requires better infrastructure, education, healthcare, market access, climate resilience, land rights, financial inclusion, good governance, and environmental conservation.

C. Osuigwe, *Economic Development of Rural Areas*, Sustainable Development Goals Series, https://doi.org/10.1007/978-3-032-10572-1_6

6.1 Introduction

This chapter explores the specific challenges to rural development in Africa, including inadequate infrastructure and limited access to quality healthcare and education. Significant attention is given to the climate impacts on agriculture, high poverty and unemployment rates, land tenure systems, and the lack of access to credit and financial support, as well as their combined impact on rural development. It also considers gender inequality, weak accountability and transparency in governance, and insufficient environmental sustainability, all of which have hindered the progress of rural development across Africa. These issues are discussed below.

6.2 Inadequate Infrastructure

One of the significant obstacles to rural development is inadequate infrastructure, including limited road networks, a lack of electricity or access to electricity, poor-quality water and sanitation that can impact health, and inadequate internet or mobile network coverage that hinders trade and marketing. All these affect economic opportunities and reduce the chances of developing the potential of rural settlements. The lack of and limited infrastructure are barriers to broad-based rural economic progress in Africa. World Bank (2009A) states that only one in three rural Africans has access to an all-season road; 20 per cent of the population in Cameroon, Ghana, Mauritania, Niger, and Tanzania travel more than two kilometres to their primary water supply; and a monthly basket of prepared mobile telephone services costs $12 in Africa but only $2 in South Asia. Osuigwe (2024) states that it is very bad news that some railway lines, which were functional when the colonialists left Africa 40 years ago, have long ceased to function. Some that are still operational are not functioning to the expected capacity. The railway lines served as a means of transporting agricultural products and linkages for rural farmers' products to consumers. Its failure to function greatly impacted rural development, particularly agriculture. This highlights the challenges of rural infrastructure in Africa, and after almost a decade and 6 years, the situation is worse than when compared to the rural population's access to basic infrastructure.

Inadequate road networks restrict access to vital services like healthcare and education, while also hampering economic growth by limiting the transportation of goods and market access. Poor infrastructure further isolates rural settlements, worsening social and economic inequalities. Additionally, lack of clean water remains a major issue in many rural parts of Africa, leaving these communities even more disadvantaged. There are efforts by international organisations in South Africa to improve access to clean water resources, but significant disparities persist, particularly in rural areas. Nigeria is a worst-case study where the government fails to provide clean water, and rural areas bear the brunt of inadequate infrastructure. Lack of water poses serious health concerns that can lead to waterborne diseases and sanitation-related illnesses, perpetuating the poverty cycle and contributing to social and economic inequality, as well as the underdevelopment of rural settlements.

The neglect of rural infrastructure is not merely an oversight but a failure to address the rural development agenda, which will increase the living standards of rural settlements and the national GDP. Jerome (2011) states that Africa's infrastructure still lags behind worldwide norms and standards in terms of both quantity and quality, despite the recognition that efficient infrastructure is a vital component for economic progress and poverty alleviation. Africa's poor and inadequate infrastructure constantly suppresses productivity and economic progress (Chakamera 2021). Inadequate infrastructural development in Africa, including road networks, telecommunications, transportation, electricity supply, water, sanitation, and internet access, discourages both domestic and international investment. This is why Azolibe and Okonkwo (2020) explained that adequate and effective infrastructure affects people's quality of life and industrialisation.

6.3 Education and Health Services Accessibility

Insufficient education and healthcare facilities in rural areas significantly hinder rural development by restricting human capital growth, limiting access to vital healthcare, and reducing residents' quality of life. Poor health infrastructure also hampers rural populations' ability to participate fully in social and economic activities. Additionally, rural schools often face resource shortages, including insufficient funding, outdated teaching materials, and a shortage of qualified teachers. Quality of education may be compromised, leading to disparities in learning outcomes between rural and urban areas (Kakupa et al., 2015).

Poor education restricts job opportunities, resulting in a lack of a skilled workforce needed for social and economic diversity and growth in rural areas. One key factor that limits community and individual participation in rural development initiatives is the poor quality of education in these areas, which affects planning, implementation, evaluation, and monitoring. Take, for example, an interview with

Ven. Ogechi Nwamadu, the Archdeacon of St. James Anglican Church, Ihitteafoukwu, on July 3, 2025, regarding the number of teachers at Town School, Ihitteafoukwu (a primary school). He states, "The primary school has only five teachers for the six levels. Primary 3 and 4 are combined in one class and taught by a single teacher". It is the same primary school where I received my primary education in the early 1980s; it had more than 18 teachers, including the headmaster and his assistant. Back then, some classes had as many as three teachers. What has happened to that same school at present? Nigeria's poor leadership, which has been deteriorating, has hurt the country's education system and hindered rural development. Imagine the consequences of combining two different classes under one teacher. The decline of rural development in many parts of Africa is also a result of poor leadership that fails to prioritise rural education.

Furthermore, limited access to healthcare results in high mortality rates, affecting the overall health and well-being of rural communities. This, in turn, influences productivity, economic growth, and development. Suppose the government fails to meet the basic needs for education and healthcare through public or private participation. In that case, it can lead to people migrating from rural areas to cities, weakening efforts to retain a skilled workforce in rural regions and hindering the success of rural development programmes and projects.

Inadequate education and limited health services in rural areas worsen existing inequalities between urban and rural populations, and in spatial terms, marginalise rural settlements. High levels of deprivation in rural regions significantly contribute to poor health outcomes (Monticelli et al., 2010). Many rural areas are further marginalised due to poor school buildings, a shortage of teachers, and a lack of libraries, facilities, and health centres. The United Nations (2020) states that low educational attainment, coupled with limited opportunities to acquire job-specific skills and on-the-job training, restricts job opportunities for many rural people seeking productive work. United nation (2020) further indicated that rural areas have fewer and less satisfactory primary care services, weaker referral systems, unsatisfactory numbers of experienced and qualified health professionals, including doctors and nurses, poorer working conditions for public health workers, inadequate social security, deficient laboratory networks and weak intersectoral action in support of health, which together undermine the health of the rural poor.

A study conducted in Poland on establishing practicable rural development action revealed that 60% of respondents emphasised the need to organise courses or training to develop local entrepreneurship (Guzal-Dec & Zwolińska-Ligaj, 2017). Bakre (2022) supported this by indicating that skills deficits remain a challenge, as a recent study established that more capacity and skills building are necessary to upscale all forms of entrepreneurs, thereby advancing both the quality and quantity of their products.

The challenges of health and education in rural Africa are a fragmentary strain that has implications for the future of rural development and the livelihood of the rural population. Insufficient education and health infrastructure and facilities, shortage of teachers, shortage of health staff, and gender disparities are collectively underscored, as well as the dire need to reform rural health and education systems. Harris (….) states that one of the most significant issues facing sub-Saharan Africa is the lack of adequate healthcare infrastructure, and many rural areas lack even basic medical facilities. Where they do exist, they are often poorly equipped and understaffed. Harris further mentioned that according to the World Health Organisation (WHO), sub-Saharan Africa has only 1.3 health workers per 1000 people, which is far below the minimum threshold of 4.5 recommended by the WHO to deliver essential health services. Another major hurdle is the shortage of healthcare professionals. Furthermore, the lack of educational materials and resources in rural African schools poses a significant challenge, as it curtails the potential for quality learning experiences, as schools often struggle to provide essential educational tools (Habib, 2018).

Addressing these challenges should focus on enhancing rural potential and improving service delivery through access to proper education and healthcare facilities. This will be evident in the key requirements for rural economic development and growth. A well-educated and healthy population in rural areas will lead to sustainable economic growth and break the cycle of poverty. Therefore, it is significant for all levels of government, local organisations, international organisations, and NGOs to assist in rural development to support the United Nations Sustainable Development Goals through good health and quality education, as explained in chapter three of this book. Transforming education and health in rural areas will change how people perceive rural settlements, encouraging investments and economic development. No one wants to invest in an area with poor health and educational facilities, and a lack of proper health and education professionals (Osuigwe, 2024).

6.4 Market

Promoting goods and services from rural areas is crucial for rural development. By providing market support, it enhances access for rural producers, helping them sell their products at fair prices and access better information, which in turn can increase their income. This also raises awareness of new technological practices.

Technology, such as the Internet, helps rural businesses market their products to a broader range of consumers. Access to a broader consumer base through the internet and mobile communications helps rural businesses avoid exploitation by middlemen.

Marketing supports rural development by communicating effectively with communities. This is achieved through community outreach, sharing information on best practices, education, healthcare services, and other relevant resources that benefit rural engagement and development. It also helps communicate the availability of new products or tools for better production or systems. Furthermore, marketing promotes rural tourism, which highlights the culture and natural resources that can attract investments.

One of the primary challenges faced by rural businesses and entrepreneurs is marketing their services and products. Furthermore, inadequate transportation systems and communication networks have posed barriers to accessibility for rural entrepreneurs and producers. Nel (2019) notes that rural producers face significant competition from urban entrepreneurs who benefit from established markets, better infrastructure, and a capital-oriented economy. Limited digital infrastructure, involving inadequate access to reliable internet connectivity, remains a significant challenge for smallholder farmers in rural areas (Sekabira & Qaim, 2017). The impact is not only on small farmers but also on all the social and economic activities in rural settlements. Tambo et al. (2019) emphasised further that limited infrastructure affects farmers' access to digital platforms and hinders the real-time exchange of data and information necessary for decision-making and market participation. It is also significant that marketing plays a crucial role in sustainable rural development planning. Without marketing, producers' chances of taking advantage of the global and regional value chains are minimal, and they will only have access to local customers, which will minimise their income. Access to regional and global value chains increases access to larger markets, leads to higher income and earnings, directly improves productivity, and enhances business operations.

6.5 Climate Change Impacts

Climate change has a significant impact on rural development, particularly in regions where weather conditions are not adequately monitored. In Africa, it impacts agriculture and other productivity sectors through unpredictable weather events such as droughts, landslides, heavy rainfall, and floods, leading to food shortages, income loss, and damage to infrastructure. Rural economies in Africa, which heavily rely on livestock, farming, and tourism, are particularly vulnerable. The effects of climate change on rural productivity exacerbate existing inequalities, as agriculture is the primary economic activity for many rural women. Additionally, it widens the urban-rural economic gap, as urban areas are often better equipped to handle climate impacts compared to rural regions.

Furthermore, it has a significant effect on crop production, which can lead to either high yields or food shortages. These shortages can cause malnutrition in rural communities, negatively affect health conditions, and reduce economic output. Climate change may also increase the frequency of pests and diseases that harm crops, as well as trigger prolonged droughts, leading to water shortages that could affect irrigation, domestic water use, and overall productivity. Additionally, climate change that disrupts rural communities and causes food shortages results in both unskilled and skilled rural-to-urban migration. The South African Department of Forestry, Fisheries, and the Environment (DFFE) has summarised the impact of climate change on rural areas, highlighting aspects that should be considered in rural development plans.

1. Declining yields from subsistence farmlands are caused by rising temperatures, unpredictable rainfall, water scarcity, and bush encroachment.
2. Decreased production of rangelands resulting from drought, bush encroachment, malnutrition, and disease.
3. Increased vulnerability to water shortages, resulting from heightened evaporation during droughts, shifts in rainfall patterns, damage to infrastructure due to floods and storm surges, and reduced groundwater recharge, impacts food production, exacerbates poverty, and drives migration.
4. Impact on natural resources that various rural communities rely on.
5. Floods and erosion caused by heavy rain and stormwater can isolate rural communities, negatively impacting their socio-economic conditions.
6. Heightened migration from rural-to-urban and peri-urban areas.

The impact of climate change can be reduced through proper monitoring and planning. This includes adopting farming practices such as drought-resistant crops and sustainable irrigation systems, encouraging rural communities to build rainwater harvesting structures, and promoting efficient water use. Governments should support rural areas with weather monitoring systems and the timely dissemination of information. Additionally, governments and other organisations need to develop policies and strategies that foster climate-resilient development. The findings of Bakre (2022) noted that the current rural development initiatives do not match the pace of resource weakening attributed to climate change. Thus, a practical plan for national drought policies is crucial for addressing such climate change. In the African rural context, climate change remains a persistent feature that requires concerted efforts by all stakeholders to navigate and address its intricate aspects; this will help implement sustainable rural development, thereby improving economic development and growth.

6.6 Land Ownership

There are four types of identified land tenure systems:

1. Privately owned land
2. Community-owned land or cooperative-owned land
3. Land owned by the government
4. Land entrusted to the community chiefs or kings

The land tenure system or land ownership in rural areas has significant implications for rural development based on who has access to land and the state of land tenure security on the title deeds. It determines the extent to which a person or entrepreneur is willing to invest in land ownership, directly affecting productivity and financial access, which in turn influences their investment decisions. An insecure land tenure system or limited access to land rights impedes rural development by discouraging long-term investments and perpetuates poverty. Security of land tenure promotes long-term investments, such as irrigation systems, infrastructure, and crop cultivation, which can take time to yield results and lead to improved production and increased income.

Land tenure or land ownership promotes sustainable rural development and directly stimulates social and economic development. Holden et al. (2011) emphasised the importance of land tenure by demonstrating how access to land leads to an increase in on-farm investment, which contributed to Ethiopia's land certification program. Security of land tenure can be used to obtain bonds, facilitate access to credit, and serve as collateral for loans; all these factors have an impact on investment, rural businesses, and the promotion of entrepreneurship in rural development. Furthermore, the security of land ownership supports food production through consistency in farming and directly impacts food security and livelihood standards. Secured tenure rights enhance the livelihoods of farmers, ensuring that their investments today will yield returns in the future (Place and Otsuka 2002).

The absence or unsustainability of land tenure systems can cause conflicts over land ownership between individuals and communities. Such disputes sometimes lead to fatalities, abandonment of land, and food shortages, which hinder rural development and result in job and investment losses. Without tenure security, rural chiefs often exploit dwellers by charging above-market rates for access to land for farming and investment. Consequently, many people migrate from rural African areas because they lack the right to own land, build properties, or invest in agriculture.

Certain African countries still uphold traditional land tenure or state ownership of land. For example, in the Ingonyama Trust in the Zulu Land of South Africa, the Zulu King acts as the trustee for the land, which is administered on behalf of specific communities. Other examples are in Namibia, where the government implements a flexible approach, providing a continuum of rights via occupancy licences and certificates of occupancy; in Ghana and Botswana, land boards made up of traditional leaders or elected officials are involved in decision-making on the implementation of the land registration process. In Nigeria, all land is owned by the government but held in trust by the citizens. What it means is that the government can take any land for development. However, this process has led to corruption, whereby government officials and political elites take land under the pretence that they will develop it for public purposes. They reallocate the same land to themselves through government sales and reissue occupancy certificates in their names. In South Africa, land use rights are based on individual ownership. However, the law stipulates that when the government requires land for development, the owner must be contacted and offered a fair price to sell the land to the government. Where the owner fails to sell the land, the government has the right to expropriate the land for its development purposes. Land rights and security of tenure are legalised through the registration of land ownership and the issuance of legal titles to the owner. However, customary land ownership could be formalised by incorporating traditional land tenure systems into the existing legal frameworks. Unsustainable land ownership in rural areas could be made legal and sustainable by redistributing land to marginalised groups that lack access to it.

6.7 Financial Exclusion

Rural development achieves sustainability only through financial inclusion, which guarantees that social and economic benefits from development efforts are accessible and enduring. Financial exclusion refers to the lack of access to formal financial services among certain rural groups. Consequently, rural communities that are excluded from the financial system due to poor planning and insufficient investment need to be financially empowered to support ongoing rural development. Financial inclusion empowers rural populations by enhancing their capabilities, promoting income-generating activities, and supporting them in managing risks associated with their livelihoods. Financial inclusion in rural areas must not only be anchored in access to credit and savings, but also in all forms of financial services that enable rural people to engage in social and economic activities. The financing exclusion gap is more pronounced in rural areas than in urban areas, and it is more severe for rural women than for rural men. Financial exclusion is highly biased in rural settlements where men have more access to financial assistance than women; it could be attributed to tradition and culture.

To highlight the significance of financial inclusion, the McKinsey Global Institute (2010) estimates that African agricultural productivity could potentially triple, increasing from USD 280 billion to USD 880 billion by 2030, if farmers gain access to finance. It is important to note that agricultural productivity is more concentrated in rural Africa than in urban areas. To ensure sustainable and inclusive economic growth, making financial inclusion in rural areas mandatory and a top priority is essential.

The exclusion of rural people from financial services significantly limits their ability to invest in their livelihoods and businesses, thereby perpetuating poverty and hindering social and economic growth. Financial exclusion not only affects business activities and agricultural production but also limits investment in infrastructure that isolates rural settlements, hindering sustainable growth and progress. A lack of financial services leads to farmers not investing in or purchasing necessary farming tools and supplies, such as fertilisers and equipment, which impact agricultural output. Furthermore, it impacts rural people's access to better education and quality healthcare, directly affecting their productivity and income.

Factors contributing to inadequate financial services in rural areas include a shortage or absence of financial institutions such as banks and microfinance services. Limited financial knowledge, information, and the capacity to develop financial proposals impede many rural populations, restricting their access to financial resources. Moreover, difficulties in obtaining financial information and crafting effective proposals prevent numerous rural entrepreneurs and businesses from securing necessary funding (Olar & Jitea, 2021). Note that financial exclusion hampers the establishment of sustainable rural development activities, relegating many initiatives to survivalist modes of operation. Furthermore, a significant obstacle to accessing financial services in rural areas is income level; many rural populations lack the funds needed to participate in financial services or the collateral required to obtain them.

Rural development policymakers and strategic planners should start considering the most effective ways to tackle financial exclusion, especially within rural communities. This can be achieved by providing small-scale loans to rural farmers through government initiatives, mobile banking solutions, and financial education for rural populations. Such actions will significantly reduce financial exclusion in rural areas and among rural dwellers.

6.8 Weak Governance Structures

A primary challenge in rural development across Africa is the inability to implement sustainable plans, mainly due to weak governance in many sub-Saharan countries. Key issues include the lack of political will and the absence of inclusive participation in planning and executing rural development projects. Additionally, low levels of accountability and transparency among government leaders hinder progress in rural areas. This lack of transparency and accountability often leads to corruption, which impedes the planning and implementation of development initiatives. Another significant barrier is the limited community involvement in development plans, as a top-down approach can weaken the effectiveness of programmes and projects. There are instances where the government imposes its ideas without consulting the communities that are supposed to benefit from these projects, which may not be well-received. This is why Nel (2019) suggests that locally driven proposals require a community-based approach, where stakeholders collectively decide on development options for their local area.

Khan (2001) pointed out that government policies can hinder rural development by unfairly penalising agriculture and neglecting rural infrastructure, which worsens rural poverty. He argued that the rural poor are a result of weak governance caused by political instability, civil conflict, discrimination based on gender, race, ethnicity, and religion, poorly defined property and land rights, and the unfair allocation of land and natural resources. Additionally, corrupt politicians, rent-seeking bureaucracies, and policies that marginalise and exclude rural populations from development efforts all contribute to this problem.

The challenges outlined are caused by weak governance structures that greatly impede rural development. These issues restrict access to services, undermine community participation, limit investments, perpetuate inequality, and lead to the mismanagement of natural resources, resulting in poverty and stagnation in rural regions. Corruption and poor governance lead to the misappropriation of funds intended for rural projects. Such corruption diverts resources from rural development efforts, impacting farmers, businesses, small-scale entrepreneurs, and light industrial developers. These groups face difficulties obtaining loans due to unclear land titles and weak financial institutions, issues that are worsened by poor governance. Additionally, an inadequate regulatory framework allows mining companies to exploit weak systems and take advantage of local populations and labour forces.

Weak governance issues can be reduced by supporting strong local institutions that operate transparently and are accountable. Such transparency and accountability establish systems to monitor and evaluate programmes and projects effectively. This is achieved by ensuring that rural populations have access to information, which helps decrease corruption and improve outcomes in rural development and economic growth. Adopting a bottom-up approach, involving rural communities from the outset, ensures the effective implementation of development plans. Good governance also fosters community participation in decision-making and resource management, while providing training that enables rural residents to contribute to policy-making and strategy development. Ultimately, this enhances rural economic development and growth.

6.9 Environmental Degradation

Scherr (1996) described environmental degradation as a decline in land's productive capacity, which can be either temporary or permanent. Gretton and Salma (1996) define land degradation as a reduction in the biological output or effectiveness of land resources used predominantly for specific purposes. Key causes include deforestation, overgrazing, land cultivation, and unsuitable agricultural practices. In Africa, the main driver of land degradation is the adoption of inappropriate farming methods. These practices include indiscriminate bush burning that damages soil properties; desertification and deforestation caused by irrational tree cutting, leading to erosion; landslides and flooding; improper irrigation systems that harm soil quality and reduce productivity; increased soil acidification, lowered water tables, and decreased fertility; poorly managed grazing systems that expose soil, damage essential plants, and cause erosion; among others (Johnson et al., 2007; Nwokoro & Chima, 2017).

Effective rural development is impossible without environmental protection, as it has a direct impact on key aspects of rural life, including access to water, food security, livelihoods, and health. This can lead to increased poverty, unemployment, migration, and social unrest. The consequences of environmental degradation are severe.

1. It could reduce the water table due to changes in climate patterns, due to farming or mining methods, or over-extraction of water for agricultural purposes. This affects the sustainability of the rural population's livelihood.
2. Poor farming practices and improper land management systems could lead to soil erosion and soil fertility, which impact crop yield and food production.
3. Environmental degradation could lead to an outbreak of diseases; this is caused by contaminated water or soil poisoning.
4. The burning of bushes could cause the loss of pollinators and beneficial species that reduce food productivity.
5. Bush burning could lead to respiratory illnesses in vulnerable populations.
6. Environmental degradation that causes damage to infrastructure and economic opportunities leads to rural-to-urban migration, creating additional challenges for rural development and the skills required.
7. Environmental degradation also leads to reduced food production, resulting in lower income, fewer employment opportunities, and increased unemployment. These factors directly impact the income of the rural population, affecting their ability to invest in education and access healthcare services.
8. Another impact of environmental degradation is the increase in floods, heatwaves, droughts, and rising sea levels, which lead to the loss of land and agricultural productivity, further impacting the income of rural populations.

Environmental degradation can be prevented through effective policies and strategies. Professionals who understand the appropriate methods can systematically reverse damage, tailored to the specific type of degradation. For example, crop rotation and agroforestry help preserve soil health by preventing erosion and other issues. Addressing nutritional deficiencies with soil amendments can overcome soil fertility problems. Rehabilitating degraded landscapes involves planting new trees and implementing civil engineering projects. Other approaches include water harvesting techniques that reduce stormwater runoff, mitigate flooding, and promote natural water use. Well-planned irrigation systems can enhance water efficiency and boost agricultural productivity. Ultimately, educating rural communities about sustainable agricultural practices will strengthen environmental protection, improve crop yields and income, and foster rural economic development.

This chapter has demonstrated how a lack of or limited infrastructure development in rural areas, combined with inadequate access to healthcare and education facilities, and restricted market access for rural products and services, pose significant challenges to sustainable rural development. Moreover, it highlighted the impact of weather and climate on productivity in rural areas, as well as the importance of climate forecasts for successful agricultural production. Land tenure or access to land ownership remains a crucial factor in rural development. Land tenure impacts investment confidence in both the short and long term; it also affects rural farmers' ability to access financial resources through bonds and collateral, which encourages and enhances rural development. Furthermore, financial exclusion is a significant obstacle to rural development, and a lack of access to finance deprives rural areas of the ability to invest and improve productivity. For proper rural economic development and growth, the rural population should be linked to sustainable financial inclusion through government grants, lower-interest loans, and access to commercial banks for everyday banking activities. Without proper financial inclusion, rural development sustainability will be a challenging strategic goal.

Weak governance has been a significant barrier to the initiation, planning, implementation, monitoring, and evaluation of rural development projects. It leads to a lack of accountability and transparency, opening the door to corruption, reducing community involvement, and undermining the success of rural initiatives. Additionally, environmental harm from unsustainable farming, poor irrigation, deforestation, and stormwater runoff leads to flooding and landslides, which damage agricultural productivity and rural livelihoods, ultimately hindering economic growth. Environmental degradation also impairs agriculture, the main economic activity in rural areas.

Growth Potentials in Rural Areas 7

Abstract

The chapter explores significant growth opportunities in rural Africa, citing abundant human and natural resources as key drivers. It highlights vast arable land, a young population, untapped resources, and rising agricultural investments as reasons why rural areas attract social and economic development. About 45% of the world's land suitable for sustainable agriculture is in Africa, making it a top global prospect. The discussion emphasises overcoming challenges through innovative strategies, developing agro-industrial production, and transitioning subsistence farmers to commercial farming. It also emphasises Africa's resource wealth—rivers, land, forests, seas, crops, minerals—and advocates for sustainable management to drive growth. It highlights sustainable tourism as a vital sector, integrating conservation to protect resources, and notes potential in traditional beverages and small-scale mining for income. Furthermore, Africa's renewable energy potential, especially solar and wind, is underscored, calling for policies to develop infrastructure and harness these resources for rural development. The chapter further suggested that sustainable forestry management emphasises responsible timber harvesting, community logging, and governance for resource sustainability. These practices support resilient ecosystems and growth by involving communities in conservation and balancing ecological and social needs. It notes Africa's rising rural purchasing power, driven by population growth, income gains, better market access, mobile tech, and the internet. This additionally enhances rural technology development by improving connectivity and information access, fostering inclusive growth. The importance of rural labour and policies addressing low wages and poor conditions is stressed, and the

C. Osuigwe, *Economic Development of Rural Areas*, Sustainable Development Goals Series, https://doi.org/10.1007/978-3-032-10572-1_7

impacts of traditional crafts are valuable for cultural preservation and economic growth, needing policies and infrastructure for market integration. The conclusion highlights rural potential and urges government support for sustainable development.

7.1 Introduction

The availability of human and natural resources is a significant growth opportunity for rural development (Osuigwe, 1996). Osuigwe emphasises that rural development in Africa can tap into the substantial potential of extensive arable land, a growing young population eager for products, unexploited natural resources, and increasing investment in agricultural technologies. These factors make rural areas in Africa appealing for social and economic opportunities and investments, despite existing challenges and risks that can be addressed. This chapter explores the potential for rural Africa, focusing on investment opportunities that can foster rural development and economic growth. These opportunities encourage stakeholders to collaborate towards social and economic improvements in rural areas and across Africa. The chapter also offers guidance on future policies and strategies for rural development.

7.2 Agricultural Potential

Given Africa's significant productive capacity, it must play a vital role in feeding the world both now and in the future. Realising this potential fully will require overcoming numerous challenges with innovative and transformative strategies. Africa holds about 45% of the world's land suitable for sustainable agricultural expansion, the largest share globally. Additionally, its low labour costs compared to other regions should be harnessed to develop labour-intensive social and economic activities. African farmers can produce many commodities at farm-level costs that are competitive internationally, partly due to the much lower average wages for unskilled workers (World Bank, 2009; Morris et al., 2009).

The future of global food production will largely depend on Africa's agricultural development and investment in its land. Africa possesses most of the world's fertile land and a large amount of uncultivated land, mainly in rural regions. Adesina (2018) emphasises this by noting that Africa has 65% of the world's unused arable land, which could serve to feed 9 billion people by 2050. Additionally, savannas comprise the largest agricultural frontier worldwide, covering approximately 400 million hectares, with only 10% of this area currently under cultivation. Africa is the world's major producer of cocoa, primarily from Côte d'Ivoire, Ghana, and Nigeria. However, it exports these products in raw form, generating little from the billions made from the global cocoa market. "Africa produces 146 million tons out of the 268 million tons of cassava in the world – or 55%, 5.4 million tons of the 5.6 million tons of cowpeas globally – or 9.62 million out of the 28 million tons of millet globally – or 43% and 29 million tons of the 69 million tons of sorghum globally - or 42%" (Adesina, 2018, p. 1). Processing these raw products into a finished form should be Africa's economic priority, as well as a means to boost rural economic growth and development.

African rural land holds the potential to significantly boost social and economic growth across the continent. However, Africa still mainly exports agricultural products as raw commodities, making it vulnerable to global commodity price swings. This underscores the need for a new focus on agro-industrial production and processing. Emphasising agro-processing and industrialisation can unlock rural potential by developing small, medium, and large-scale commercial farms. To mitigate the continent's stagnated development challenges, this book suggests that Africa should start charting a way forward through commercialising rural farming. The continent has had hard-working farmers trapped in poverty for centuries due to the practice of subsistence farming. To change the narrative is to assist them through a well-designed agricultural strategic development system that will transform them from subsistence farmers to commercial farmers.

There are significant obstacles to unlocking the agricultural potential of rural areas, mainly due to a lack of political will to implement effective policies and strategies. If these challenges were addressed, the continent's agricultural capabilities could be fully exploited for economic growth. This could be achieved through expanding agricultural production possibilities by removing constraints via regulation, improving infrastructure in rural areas, developing transportation networks, enhancing access to the internet and mobile networks to connect farmers with regional and global value chains, increasing the use of technology in rural areas, and improving access to financial services such as credit and grants for farmers.

To improve the agricultural potential of rural settlements and communities, the government should shift the narrative of inequalities in rural areas, where women often face difficulties in owning land and properties in many African countries. Africa cannot achieve economic sustainability without ensuring women's full and equal participation in the economy. There should be an improvement in women's access to economic opportunities, particularly in rural areas where the burden of inequality is severe, as women often bear the responsibility for agricultural production. Therefore, reducing the gender gap in agriculture could be achieved by engaging women and youth in the sector and providing them with greater access to agricultural facilities.

It is troubling that African countries spend billions on importing food every year, despite the continent having some of the most fertile and uncultivated land in the world. Adesina (2028) supported this point by stating that there is no reason why Africa spends US$35 billion annually on food imports. Africa must utilise available technologies and implement appropriate policies, which will lead to rapidly increasing agricultural productivity and farmers' incomes, while also ensuring lower food prices for consumers.

For agricultural potential to be fully realised, access to financial services must improve. Government-run agricultural development banks need to operate professionally and avoid being influenced by politics or elites, as such influences can lead to corruption and impede their ability to support agricultural growth, especially in rural areas. Additionally, rural and commercial farmers—mainly based in rural regions—depend heavily on private banks that charge very high and unsustainable lending rates. This is an area where the government should collaborate with the private sector to make agricultural investment more appealing through effective policies.

In the continent, rural economies—centred on agricultural innovation and technology—are vital for overcoming economic struggles. These rural areas hold the greatest potential to elevate the continent from underdevelopment. The book advocates that revitalising rural economies will address economic issues and alleviate associated challenges. This can be done through rural agricultural development, encouraging young, entrepreneurial female farmers to emerge. The outcomes will include more job opportunities, a revitalised rural economy, and less rural-to-urban migration.

Consider this: Africa's food and agribusiness market is projected to be worth an impressive $1 trillion by 2030 (Adesina, 2028). Furthermore, reflect on the following points: Africa has the largest share of arable land, the most extensive water resources, a significant pool of unskilled labour for farming, abundant agricultural and natural resources ready for development, a vast potential market for agricultural products, and ample opportunities to enhance agricultural technology and innovation. In addition, there are strong prospects for transforming traditional agriculture into commercially viable farming. Africa holds the key to the world's food basket; so, what is preventing Africa from realising this potential?

7.3 Natural Resources

Africa's rural regions are rich in natural resources, offering significant economic prospects for the continent's growth. These resources—such as rivers, land, forests, seas, oceans, crops, mining sites, and beverage potential—are vital to economic development. Exploiting these resources responsibly can promote sustainable growth and uplift rural communities. Developing effective policies and strategies for resource management will enable rural areas to adopt sustainable practices, thereby enhancing both economic and social well-being. This can be supported through targeted investments in agriculture, renewable energy, and tourism. To fully harness rural potential, environmental conservation must be sustainable, and residents should benefit directly from these resources. This section highlights key natural resources in rural areas, including tourism, beverages, mining, crafts, renewable energy, and sustainable forestry.

7.3.1 Tourism

Sustainable tourism development should address the needs of both tourists and the host community while protecting and improving future opportunities. It involves managing resources to meet economic, social, and aesthetic goals, all while preserving cultural integrity, ecological systems, biological diversity, and vital life support systems (World Tourism Organisation (UNWTO, 2010). Additionally, Sebunya (2024) highlights that Africa is on the verge of transformation, with tourism acting as a catalyst for economic growth and sustainable progress. The continent's natural resources—mainly located in rural areas—such as landscapes, wildlife, and cultural heritage, are crucial attractions and fundamental to building an inclusive, resilient economy. Sebunya (2024) also notes that tourism plays a significant role in Africa's economy, generating around $170 billion annually and employing 24 million people. By developing rural tourism infrastructure, investments will increase, income will rise, jobs will be created, and new opportunities will emerge.

To support the potential for tourism growth and sustainable rural development, rural areas should focus on conserving natural resources that attract visitors. Africa's rural regions boast rich wildlife, historical and cultural artefacts, traditional relics, diverse ecosystems, and breathtaking landscapes. These assets play a crucial role in driving tourism, which in turn fosters economic growth. Sustainable rural tourism development should be supported by policies and strategies that are integrated with conservation, ensuring that tourism growth aligns with the conservation of the continent's natural wealth. Tourism anchored on conservation offers prospects for the rural population to benefit directly from the protection of their natural surroundings. Tourism development is affixed on conservation, nurturing a sense of ownership while providing job opportunities and improving livelihoods.

To unlock tourism potential in rural regions, policies should focus on community-based tourism enterprises, promote cultural and traditional activities, improve rural infrastructure, enhance skills training for local populations, and foster regional partnerships to develop accessible travel routes across Africa. Lankford et al. (2008) note that tourism thrives in peaceful settings and can also contribute to peacebuilding and positive change at individual, community, national, and international levels.

Africa's rural tourism potential is diverse, encompassing unique biodiversity that supports community-led wildlife viewing, exploration of natural landscapes, animal watching, hiking, and ecotourism activities such as water sports, canoeing, and fishing. It also involves cultural and traditional experiences through relics, artefacts, crafts, music, dance, and storytelling, as well as visits to archaeological, ancient, and heritage sites. To make these resources successful, it is essential to develop adequate infrastructure, involve local communities, promote sustainable tourism practices, simplify visa processes for regional and international visitors, and offer training in tourism skills and development for rural communities.

7.3.2 Beverages

A key challenge for African leadership is understanding how rural populations perceive their community. Their perception reflects their identity, rooted in their culture and way of life. These cultural aspects influence what they eat and drink. Strengthening these cultures can support social and economic development and growth. Osuigwe (2024) states that Western and Asian leaders have developed some of their cultural features and ideas that led to the manufacturing of goods and services that dominate the world; he gave examples such as the Ireland Guinness, American Coca-Cola, McDonald, Pepsi, beers, and different forms of alcoholic brands, as well as Russian Gins and Whiskies. As stated earlier in this paragraph, culture encompasses the foods and beverages people consume; in each ethnic group in Africa, there are indigenous beers, wines, and gins that are locally produced. These beverages can potentially develop in rural areas, as many of them are traditionally consumed in these regions. Osuigwe (2024) listed the following beverages, as shown in Table 7.1 below.

Table 7.1 Examples of Gin, Alcohol, and Wine in Africa

Name of the Beer	The Country or region of origin
Tombo (palm wine) in Nigeria is known as Nsafufuo in Ghana, and it has various names in other west African countries.	West Africa
Mgonbotho and Marula (beer)	Southern Africa
Ogogoro, Kai-Kai, apetesi (gin)	Nigeria
Pombe (beer)	East Africa
Dolo, Pito, Shukutu, Burukutu, and Tchakpalo (beer)	West Africa
Bouza	Ethiopia and Egypt
Merisa (beer)	Sudan and southern Sudan
Marva	Uganda
Ubuki	Rwanda
Talla (wine), Korefe, shamit, tej, and Arik (beers)	Ethiopia
Maujek and Chang'aa (beer)	Kenya
Mowa (beer)	Malawi
Apheteshie (gin)	Ghana

Source Osuigwe (2024)

These indigenous drinks hold great potential for rural development. Investing in proper infrastructure and financial services could stimulate innovation in traditional beverages, leading to more job creation, entrepreneurship, and overall social and economic growth. Osuigwe (2024) notes that traditional refining methods for these alcoholic beverages face marketing challenges. Therefore, the most effective strategy would be to refine the process and develop strong branding to meet international standards and enhance market appeal. If African traditional beer can be refined with an appealing taste and effective branding, the industry could employ many people, thereby reducing African unemployment and poverty rates (Osuigwe, 2024). Europeans and Asians have successfully transformed their traditional alcoholic drinks and wines into global brands.

For these products to expand and become part of the global value chain, government encouragement and support are essential. The government should create effective policies and strategies that facilitate both domestic and foreign investment in this potential.

> "The rejection of indigenous knowledge and brews in favour of Western beverages is a mistake that needs to be corrected. To preserve the indigenous knowledge of producing brews, experts should be recognised, and the invention of modern technology should not be seen as a threat to the indigenous production of indigenous brews; rather, it should be used positively to advance the mass production of indigenous brews. It is important to have local people producing their traditional brews using modern technology. This will help integrate local brews into the national/international market, and most importantly, it will ensure that the knowledge that was previously used to satisfy the spiritual and material needs of local people is documented. This will effectively use, preserve and promote the indigenous method of making beverages" (Shokane et al., 2016)

Many African countries are not fully leveraging their potential for rural development and economic growth. To remedy this, effective policies, strategies, and government support are necessary at various levels. These measures will help develop rural regions and stimulate economic growth across many African nations.

7.3.3 Small-Scale Mining

In the last two decades, small-scale mining has emerged as a labour-intensive mineral extraction activity, solidifying its position as one of the most significant sources of rural income in Africa. Moreover, it has helped improve food security, create jobs, and enhance economic resilience in many vulnerable rural communities. Although small-scale miners rely heavily on it for generating income, they still struggle to get licences from government authorities. They also face hurdles in securing funding, obtaining loans, and accessing technology that can make mining more efficient. The mining sector plays a crucial role in advancing economic development, underscoring its importance in sub-Saharan Africa (Hausermann et al., 2018). Most rural small-scale mining is informal, unregulated, and largely unsustainable due to a lack of policy direction and inadequate government support for rural development. Inappropriate policy and licensing frameworks have, in effect, fostered the informality that now characterises artisanal and small-scale mining (ASM) in sub-Saharan Africa (Traoré et al., 2024). The estimated employment by small-scale mining in Sub-Saharan Africa is shown in some selected African countries in Table 7.2 below.

The potential of small-scale mining is evident from the data in Table 7.2. It operates at such a high rate that it plays a crucial role in boosting Africa's economy and creating jobs. Engaging local communities in the formulation of policies

Table 7.2 Estimated ASM employment figures in selected African countries

Country	Country Classification (Income Group)	Data Year	Estimated number of people employed directly in ASM	Estimated number of people dependent on ASM	Major commodities mined on an artisanal and small scale
Burkina Faso	Low	2017	1,000,000	6,000,000	Gold
Burundi	Low	2014	60,000.	360,000	Gold, 3 T
DR Congo	Low	2017	2,000,000	12,000,000	Gold, diamond, 3 T, cobalt, and copper
Ghana	Low-middle	2016	1,200,000	7,200,000	Gold, diamond, salt and sand
Guinea	Low	2016	350,000	2,100,000	Gold and diamond
Madagascar	Low	2017	500,000	3,000,000	Gold and coloured gemstone
Mali	Low	2016	500,000	3,000,000	Gold
Mozambique	Low	2017	100,000	600,000	Gold and coloured gemstone
Niger	Low	2021	600,000	3,600,000	Gold
Nigeria	Low-middle	2017	400,000	2,400,000	Gold, industrial minerals
Tanzania	Low-middle	2015	1,000,000	6,000,000	Gold, coloured gemstones
Uganda	Low	2018	300,000+	1,800,000+	Gold
Zambia	Low	2017	35,000+	210,000+	Coloured gemstones, gold
Zimbabwe	Low-middle	2015	1,000,000	6,000,000	Gold, chromite, lithium

Source Traoré et al. (2024)

and strategies can significantly transform rural areas. These policies should focus on minimising environmental and social harms through well-designed measures. Developing small-scale mining in rural regions offers employment opportunities that enhance income and livelihoods, fostering economic growth. When well-managed, small-scale mining can promote infrastructure development, benefiting rural communities and attracting investments in areas such as financial services, education, and healthcare. In rural regions, it fosters entrepreneurial initiatives and sparks innovation, encouraging local markets for agricultural goods and various services. Studies indicate that small-scale mining in Africa's rural areas helps develop skills and provides training, empowering local populations economically and creating more job opportunities.

A significant challenge for small-scale mining in rural areas is the lack of effective regulation. This often results in environmental issues, such as pollution, deforestation, and land degradation, which negatively impact agricultural productivity and the livelihoods of local workers. Sometimes, unregulated mining also leads to community conflicts that damage property, services, and infrastructure. However, establishing a strong regulatory framework, combined with effective policies and strategies, can support sustainable mining practices that foster social and economic development. Engaging local communities in mining projects can improve their sustainability. Moreover, providing training enhances skills and income, promoting stability and growth in rural regions. With thoughtful planning and community involvement, rural mining can become a driver of sustainable economic progress when conducted responsibly and sustainably.

7.3.4 Renewable Energy

Africa possesses extensive renewable energy potential, covering diverse regions with solar, wind, biomass, and hydropower resources. Solar power is available across all African countries and offers significant potential. Wind energy is more prevalent in the northern, western, and southern areas. Geothermal energy is concentrated along the Great Rift Valley, particularly in West African nations. Overall, solar energy is accessible throughout Africa and tends to be more cost-effective compared to other renewable energy sources. These energy resources, especially solar and wind, can be readily utilised for rural development. However, the lack of access to other untapped alternative energy sources remains a significant reason for the ongoing energy crisis on the continent, impeding rural economic progress and growth. Strengthening the provision of green energy in rural areas will boost the continent's economic strength. The lack of energy affects the capacity to pump water for irrigation purposes, which is crucial for rural agricultural development. Inadequate energy infrastructure in rural Sub-Saharan Africa has been a persistent poverty trap, triggering cyclical famines and jeopardising local development opportunities (Osabohien et al., 2019).

By utilising renewable energy sources like solar and wind in Africa's rural areas, we can supply electricity to local businesses, residents, industries, and services. This approach will promote job creation, economic development, and progress. Solar and wind power can be systematically planned and implemented to support rural grid infrastructure, thereby enhancing economic growth and providing better access to essential services, including healthcare, education, and improving overall quality of life.

Solar and wind energy systems can be scaled down easily, making them perfect for providing electricity to rural settlements and creating sustainable social and economic opportunities. Embracing solar and wind energy will promote decentralised energy systems and make maintenance easier, benefiting both domestic and international investors. Training local people in rural areas to install, maintain, and operate solar and wind energy systems is one of the most promising avenues for rural development. For example, in southeastern Nigeria, some young people have received training in solar energy installation and maintenance, making them available to individuals who want to install solar energy systems in their homes and businesses. The take-up of renewable energy in rural southeastern Nigeria is primarily driven by the unreliable energy supply from the regional energy industry, rather than being part of a government-planned programme or project. Instead, it is a grassroots initiative driven by individuals.

Solar and wind energies have the potential to employ thousands of people if fully utilised. These types of renewable energy promise higher energy conversion from sunlight and wind, resulting in greater energy efficiency and lower costs for rural commercial, agricultural, industrial, and residential consumers. New technologies are also being developed for novel applications, for instance, building-integrated photovoltaics (BIPV) create products that serve as building components while simultaneously generating electricity, such as roofs or façades. It has been proven that solar and wind energies can be applied to industrial processes, such as water desalination, enhanced oil recovery, food processing, and mineral processing. African governments should harness solar and wind energy to bridge the energy provision gap.

Supporting the development of wind and solar energy in rural areas through government policies and strategies is crucial for sustainable growth. By tapping into Africa's renewable energy potential, opportunities for energy access will emerge, driving technological innovation and making a significant contribution to rural development (Gondo, 2010). Initiatives focusing on rural renewable energy will bring reliable electricity to rural communities, promoting social and economic progress, and enhancing the livelihoods and incomes of those living in these areas.

7.3.5 Sustainable Forestry Management

Africa's forests cover approximately 635 million hectares, constituting 16.8 per cent of the world's forest cover. The continent's forests are classified into nine main categories: tropical rainforests, tropical moist forests, tropical dry forests, tropical shrublands, tropical mountain forests, subtropical humid forests, subtropical dry forests, subtropical mountain forests, and plantations (Gondo, 2010, p. 10). In many countries, forests are vital for economic resources, with the tropical wood trade accounting for an average of 6 per cent of GDP and 10 per cent of foreign trade in the Congo Basin nations (FAO, 2009). Across Southern and East Africa, forests made up 21.4% of the relative income share, whereas crops accounted for 32.2%. Products from trees on farms also play a vital role in supporting livelihoods throughout Africa (Angelsen et al., 2014). Fruit trees serve as a substantial source of income and a direct source of nutrition for many families. For instance, research from Uganda, based on data from a national survey of nearly 1400 households over 10 years, found that households which expanded the area dedicated to trees on their farms, especially fruit trees, experienced a notable rise in their total consumption (Miller et al., 2020).

Adopting sustainable forestry management practices encourages responsible timber use, supports community-based logging that boosts income, and helps conserve biodiversity. Kufakwandi (2000) observed that in many African nations, economic activities focus on basic needs and often lack the capacity for long-term planning, which is crucial for successful sustainable forestry initiatives. Therefore, a sustainable forestry approach is essential for developing rural African areas, ensuring forest resources are used responsibly to sustain local livelihoods. Such strategies can provide multiple benefits, including income generation, energy supplies, and building materials. By improving access to better forestry management, communities can also reap environmental benefits, such as ecosystem management, which helps prevent degradation and deforestation. A successful, sustainable forestry management system for rural development should promote community-based management, develop programmes that deliver direct benefits from forest products, and establish a plan for forestry conservation.

Practical sustainable forestry should support integrated methods that produce timber while enhancing soil health and biodiversity. Efficient wood harvesting is essential to prevent deforestation. A wood management system can be a key strategy for rural development as part of a forestry management programme or project. The sustainable forest management plan should also promote rural timber processing industries, boosting economic growth, attracting investment, increasing income, and fostering overall prosperity. Forestry can also provide food sources like fruits and nuts, helping to combat food scarcity and encourage healthy living. Community forestry management in rural areas can aid in conserving biodiversity and protecting water resources. Furthermore, the forestry management programme should involve communities actively, promoting economic sustainability.

Although there are potential benefits, Africa faces significant hurdles in adopting sustainable forestry practices due to inadequate regulatory systems and a lack of transparency in forestry management. Moreover, an unclear land tenure system leads to conflicts between individuals and communities, often resulting in property loss. The absence of skills and financial services also hampers the effective management of sustainable rural forestry. Therefore, effective governance of the forestry management system is crucial for the sustainable use of forestry resources, which in turn will drive economic development in rural areas.

7.4 African Rural Market

There is considerable potential for increased buying power in Africa's rural areas, primarily due to a growing population and rising disposable income resulting from lower expenses, particularly in fast-moving consumer goods. However, its buying power is limited by restricted access to formal markets and limited access to mobile communication and the internet. The purchasing power of Africa's middle class is expected to rise significantly in the coming years, with the continent's middle class forecast to spend \$2.1 trillion by 2025 and \$2.5 trillion by 2030 (Signe, 2018). This highlights the importance and potential of the African market, with most of this purchasing power concentrated in rural areas, as well as the connections between urban residents and their rural communities. Many urban residents send billions of pounds to their villages or rural areas each month to support their relatives living there, known as the "Black Tax". This regular financial support boosts consumer spending power in rural areas.

A key driver of market potential in rural areas is the increasing population, which in turn raises demand for goods and services. This trend is especially clear in Africa, where rural populations surpass urban ones. Another contributor is the growth of the middle class, supported by new infrastructure that attracts more domestic and foreign investments. Additionally, better internet access opens more opportunities for demand. The prevalent high-level, informal market, along with local market structures, also presents significant opportunities for businesses to tap into rural consumer spending. A new class of consumers is emerging in Africa, particularly within the middle class, who are drawn to products from other nations due to their youth and upward mobility (Osuigwe, 2024). This class also seeks out youth-oriented consumer products, potentially leading to the commercialisation of rural areas and the production of certain goods and services.

Despite the potential of rural disposal income, it is limited by low overall disposable income. Introducing e-commerce in rural areas faces significant hurdles, such as resource scarcity, knowledge gaps, and affordability challenges. Often, rural regions lack essential infrastructure like reliable internet, which is necessary for e-commerce development. Nonetheless, policy and strategy makers can play a crucial role in addressing these issues, enabling rural communities and Africa to harness substantial economic gains. This can help rural producers, service providers, and consumers access global markets, boost production, connect to business opportunities more easily, and reduce advertising costs. In turn, these policies will enhance living standards for rural populations and foster economic growth. Furthermore, the population and density of many rural African areas are very high, and the low disposable income has little implication for spending behaviour. Recognising the needs of rural consumers is crucial for creating a business plan. Additionally, in some rural areas, disposable income is often spent on essential food items, personal care products, household goods, and access to microfinance services, basic healthcare services, and medication.

Many rural areas still heavily rely on farming, with farmers continually searching for seedlings, fertilisers, animal feed, and market connections for their produce. Concurrently, these regions are keen to adopt green energy sources like solar power, as many utilities face challenges in providing reliable electricity. By creating more effective plans and strategies, these opportunities can be harnessed to promote rural development. For example, increasing agricultural output to meet local demands and serve regional markets can have a meaningful impact. Improving existing distribution networks and expanding local markets will also play a crucial role, encourage entrepreneurship, and create jobs. Enhanced internet access will support digital marketing, raise income levels, increase disposable income, and ultimately foster rural growth.

7.5 Technology and Innovations

Technology and innovation are essential for rural growth, providing solutions to enhance infrastructure, increase economic chances, and empower communities via access to communication, information, education, and healthcare. Many rural African regions now have internet and mobile connectivity, which strengthens communication networks and opens opportunities for economic progress and growth. These technological improvements are crucial for upgrading services like education, healthcare, and information sharing, helping to close the digital divide and support inclusive development in rural areas. However, Seuyong et al. (2023) note that a significant digital divide exists between rural and urban Africans. In urban areas, internet access stands at 47%, whereas in rural areas, it is only 12%. The report further indicates that, as a result, computer access is also considerably lower in rural regions compared to urban ones. "While urban residents enjoy a 21% computer access rate, rural residents have only a 3.5% rate. In contrast, the difference in phone access between urban and rural residents is much smaller. In urban areas, 86% of Africans have access to a phone, whereas in rural areas, this rate is 69%" (Seuyong et al., 2023). Nevertheless, there are numerous rural areas in Africa with high access to the internet and mobile phones. For instance, in many parts of southeastern Nigeria, mobile networks and the internet are widely accessible. Similarly, in many rural areas of South Africa, internet and mobile networks are available. Access to the internet and mobile networks could drive technology and innovation in these areas.

Technology and innovation, driven by better internet and mobile network access, have enormous potential to boost rural development. By improving access to information and enhancing farming practices, they can make a real difference. Moreover, internet and mobile accessibility create more market opportunities, allowing farmers and businesses to sell their products and services to a broader market and connect them to global, regional, and local market chains. This, in turn, empowers local businesses, provides quality education, and enhances the quality of life in rural communities. If properly managed, the internet and mobile networks can also increase online learning and telehealth services.

Rural areas with internet and mobile access can utilise video calls and phone conversations to seek advice on local issues. This improves the services offered by mobile clinics, resulting in better health outcomes, which then increase productivity and income. Mobile banking apps also help people save money and access a range of financial services, boosting their economic engagement. Additionally, technology and innovation allow rural communities to receive real-time updates on weather conditions.

The main obstacle to technology and innovation is illiteracy. However, just a day or two of training can teach rural communities how to effectively use new technologies. This can boost their skills, increase productivity, and raise disposable income. Investing in better internet and mobile networks will further support technological growth in rural areas and foster sustainable development. Technological progress must be inclusive, ensuring all rural businesses, workers, and employers benefit. They must be accessible and affordable, and investment in rural connectivity and skills development should be a top priority (ILO, 2023).

7.6 Labour

Labour is fundamental to development; thus, rural labour plays a vital role in rural progress. In these areas, labour underpins the economy through farming, trade, and small-scale industries like manufacturing and mining. Most of Africa's agricultural output is generated by rural workers. This boosts incomes, fights poverty, enhances food security, raises living standards, and drives overall national growth. Since rural regions produce most of Africa's food, rural labour is critical for maintaining food security, especially with the increasing global food demand (ILO, 2023). Furthermore, rural areas host various economic activities—such as commerce, farming, tourism, and manufacturing—that attract investment and foster local skill development.

Many rural regions in Africa serve as centres of agricultural output, depending on farming, livestock, and fishing for food production. Rural workers are crucial for these sectors, supplying essential skills—especially for unskilled labour—in roles like infrastructure development, community initiatives, and facility building. Additionally, they contribute significantly to tourism services by providing valuable knowledge and skills for sustainable resource management.

The primary challenge facing rural labour is discouraging workers from remaining in their communities and promoting migration to cities. This is mainly caused by low wages and poor working conditions, which negatively impact their quality of life and hinder rural development. According to the ILO (2020), about 28 million rural workers in Africa (21% of wage earners) earn below the minimum wage. Additionally, Pahle (2015) observed that rural workers in Africa are often poorly organised, with few opportunities for collective bargaining and free association, leading to low pay. Rural workers typically earn significantly less than their urban counterparts, partly because many jobs are seasonal, resulting in unstable income and increased unemployment during peak periods. A lack of educational qualifications also plays a role in low wages, which often fail to meet the minimum standards set by many African countries. Rural labour is crucial for rural development, supporting sectors like agriculture, trade, tourism, manufacturing, and construction. These sectors contribute to the country's GDP growth, generate income for rural residents, and improve the overall quality of life in rural communities.

7.7 Rural Craft

Traditional crafts are predominantly found in rural areas of Africa, and their promotion in urban markets is vital for maintaining the cultural identity of these communities. Rural crafts act as a bridge across generations, highlighting the skills and creativity of master artisans. Craftsmanship is more than a mere product; it represents a heritage handed down through the ages, offering economic opportunities while conserving cultural traditions. The evolution of cultural crafts can generate employment opportunities, attract tourists, and enhance the quality of life for residents. Kerr (1990) notes that a stable, non-agricultural lifestyle that supports handicraft traditions can significantly enhance the sustainability of rural livelihoods. Pye (1988) suggests that over 2.18 million people in India are employed full-time in craft, contributing to foreign exchange earnings and generating revenue from the export of artisan-produced handicrafts, which account for 16 per cent of India's total trade and 13 per cent of Nepal's.

There is a significant shortfall in support for rural crafts from African policymakers and strategic developers across all levels of government. The handicraft sector in Africa needs to be developed to enable effective engagement with the government, which in turn will encourage job creation and improve the livelihoods of rural populations, particularly those with limited access to technology. Handicrafts require minimal technology, apart from marketing.

Traditional crafts in rural Africa have played a vital role in preserving cultural heritage, providing a steady income for generations, creating jobs, empowering local communities, and promoting sustainable economic growth. Crafts that have endured for centuries are dynamic tools for diversifying the social and economic landscape of rural areas. In rural settings, crafts have enabled many residents to become self-employed, reducing their reliance on other employment sources. Many unique crafts have also become a key source of tourism activities, boosting employment and local economies. Through craft tourism, cultural heritage is preserved, traditional stories and practices are passed down through generations, and social and economic interaction is fostered, strengthening community engagement and bonds.

Crafts can significantly enhance rural development, but their success depends on implementing appropriate policies, strategic planning, and infrastructure to maximise their benefits. This includes providing practical training, upgrading facilities, and launching marketing campaigns. A thriving craft industry must be connected to global, regional, and local value chains while preserving the ecosystems it has nurtured for generations. Establishing an online marketplace for artisans can help them reach a broader audience and sell directly to consumers, thereby eliminating the need for middlemen. Developing a strong brand identity for rural crafts and utilising the internet, mobile technology, and social media can increase awareness and demand both locally and internationally. Market structures created through rural development plans should promote partnerships with community organisations, government agencies, and educational institutions to provide training workshops, improve artisans' skills, and keep them updated with current design trends. Craft development also helps preserve traditional skills and knowledge, supporting a sustainable economy that utilises local resources responsibly. Community participation and engagement are essential for the long-term success of craft development.

7.8 Environmental and Biodiversity

As Africa's population continues to grow, inadequate rural development planning and policies could threaten the environment and biodiversity. It is well known that biodiversity is essential for maintaining resilient and healthy ecosystems, which support our food, energy, and water resources, as well as efforts to adapt to and mitigate climate change, ultimately ensuring human survival. Biodiversity provides raw materials for food and feed, construction, clothing, crafts, medicines, and many other uses, including daily necessities (Cámara-Leret & Dennehy, 2019). "Ecotourism supports communities to conserve biodiversity, increase their livelihoods and food security. Communities become custodians of biodiversity, taking advantage of biodiversity management approaches such as protected areas" (FAO, 2020). One of the significant challenges faced by most countries in sub-Saharan Africa is reducing poverty among rural households and protecting the ecosystems and biodiversity that these households rely on for their basic needs, such as subsistence agriculture, safe drinking water, and forest products (FAO, 2020). Furthermore, in the rapidly evolving field of sustainable development, community engagement has become a key driver of meaningful change.

Central to sustainable development is empowering local communities, as their strong connection to the environment makes them key conservation partners.

When communities participate in tree-planting and forest management efforts, it fosters a sense of ownership and helps ensure these projects succeed in the long run. Additionally, involving community members allows projects to benefit from their indigenous knowledge, resources, and cultural practices, enhancing conservation outcomes. FAO & UNEP (2020) state that ensuring positive outcomes for both biodiversity and people requires a careful balance between conservation goals and demands for resources that support livelihoods and the needs of the rural people.

Many rural communities preserve invaluable indigenous and cultural values within their ecosystems. These may include native species and sustainable land management techniques that have been passed down through generations for centuries, promoting conservation and biodiversity-focused tourism. By involving the community, biodiversity and environmental protection can become sustainable, fostering a sense of environmental responsibility and helping to preserve natural habitats.

Community-based ecotourism initiatives that engage local communities in planning, managing, and sharing the benefits of tourism activities foster a sense of responsibility and ownership over natural resources. It will help alleviate poverty, ease pressure on fragile ecosystems, and preserve local cultures and heritage. For example, good biodiversity projects that are put into action in South Africa's biodiversity economy node concept are

1. The Greater Addo to Amathole node in the Eastern Cape Province,
2. The Greater Kruger-Limpopo node in Limpopo Province, and
3. The Greater-iSimangaliso node in KwaZulu-Natal Province.

The World Bank (2021, A) states that the biodiversity economy is central to South Africa's tourism industry and building the resilience of communities to climate change. Empowering communities to invest in the biodiversity economy will create jobs, promote biodiversity stewardship, and stimulate rural development in a climate-smart way", thus was said by Marie Françoise Marie Nelly, World Bank Country Director for South Africa, Botswana, Eswatini, Lesotho, and Namibia.

Rural areas hold significant potential but realising it requires careful planning and management. These potential spans agriculture, natural resources (such as tourism, beverages, mining, biodiversity, and forestry), rural markets, technology and innovation, crafts, and labour. Achieving this potential depends on government intervention through effective policies and strategies for sustainable rural development. The next chapter will examine the role of governments in planning and implementing rural development initiatives.

8 Examinations of Government and Community Role in Rural Development

Abstract

The chapter explores the roles and frameworks of private sectors, public entities, NGOs, and communities in rural development. It stresses the significance of policies, regulations, strategies, initiatives, and plans in managing programmes, projects, and monitoring progress. The text emphasises the vital involvement of both government and communities in providing infrastructure, funding, policy frameworks, and overseeing planning and execution. It is organised into sections that cover various aspects of rural development, such as community and village organisation as key drivers of sustainability, highlighting their contributions to social welfare, environmental sustainability, and cultural preservation. The role of local, state/provincial, and national governments is examined, with local governments providing essential services, supporting local economies, and encouraging community participation. State and provincial departments coordinate projects, allocate resources, foster economic growth, and facilitate access to land and infrastructure. National governments develop comprehensive policies and strategies for rural development. The chapter also discusses initiatives by communities, local, state/provincial, and national governments aimed at promoting sustainable rural communities. Overall, the document emphasises the need for strong partnerships between private investors, governments, communities, and NGOs to promote sustainable programmes and projects. It also points out challenges faced by rural organisations, including limited government funding, political interference, and leadership gaps. The text recommends that government support, via effective policies, leadership development, and technological advances, can help address these issues.

C. Osuigwe, *Economic Development of Rural Areas*, Sustainable Development Goals Series, https://doi.org/10.1007/978-3-032-10572-1_8

Keywords

Community • Development • Policy and strategy

8.1 Introduction

This chapter explores the government and community frameworks that influence rural development. These frameworks are responsible for creating policies, regulations, strategies, initiatives, and plans, as well as managing programmes and projects, and monitoring and evaluating progress. Governments play a crucial role by providing infrastructure, funding, policy frameworks, and overseeing planning and implementation. Communities contribute their knowledge, labour, and leadership to ensure programmes address their specific needs, fostering sustainable social and economic growth in rural areas. Successful rural development relies on strong partnerships among private investors, governments, communities, and NGOs to form alliances that support sustainable programmes and projects. The focus on government and community roles stems from their essential roles; without effective structures, rural development cannot succeed. These roles and structures are detailed below.

8.2 Community or Village Organisation

Community and village organisations are the key drivers of sustainable rural development, providing essential support, expertise, and human resources. They promote an inclusive and equitable governance approach that is vital for success. These organisations support social welfare, environmental sustainability, and cultural preservation, which are all crucial for meaningful development. Additionally, they contribute unique indigenous knowledge that development experts might lack, helping to promote sustainable growth. An example of a typical rural organisation is shown in the organogram below, based on a study conducted at Ihitteaforukwu in Ahiazu Mbaise Local Government Area, Imo State, Nigeria. Traditional authorities also play a critical role in addressing challenges and fostering sustainable rural development.

Figure 8.1 displays the Ihitteaforukwu Community Town Union Organogram, which has guided the community's development over the past 45 years. This town union is important because its executives are elected for a maximum of four years, after which new leadership takes over. All heads of the community town union's subsections are also elected, except for the Clan head, who is chosen based on the age of the oldest male in the clan. The other positions are all elected. The women's association promotes balanced gender participation, although they often contribute to discussions in the general assembly. This town union and its subordinate organisation have helped the community to implement various projects, including electricity, clinics, roads, community halls, and water initiatives, and have also addressed security issues in the villages that form the community.

Rural organisations are crucial for development, acting as platforms for transparent and responsible governance that involve rural communities in decision-making and project execution. Various government agencies, private developers, institutions, and NGOs collaborate with them to implement programmes and initiatives. These organisations serve as grassroots catalysts for initiating, planning, and executing projects, supporting rural infrastructure development by lobbying for essential projects and empowering locals through training and assistance. Some rural groups facilitate the formation of cooperatives in agriculture, SMEs, and other sectors, promoting microfinance institutions that offer credit and technical support, thereby driving rural entrepreneurship, job creation, and economic growth. In Ihitteaforukwu, the town union has mobilised the community multiple times to address social and economic challenges, notably during the COVID-19 pandemic, when many donated foods to be distributed in villages. They also supported small businesses with small grants allocated via community organisations, although monitoring their success and impact remains a challenge.

Many rural organisations enhance service delivery by building or offering facilities like local clinics, schools, libraries, and other infrastructure that support rural businesses and agriculture. This includes rural marketplaces, irrigation systems, and farm seedlings. Some community groups also help maintain rural roads and install streetlights to improve the area's appearance and safety. These efforts have led to job creation, lower illiteracy rates, better rural health, and have directly contributed to reducing poverty, fostering economic growth, and encouraging development.

Several rural organisations in the region actively promote forestry conservation and environmental sustainability. For instance, in Umuoni Village of Ihittaforukwu Community, the community safeguards the Nnenke Stream ecosystem by banning tree-cutting activities. Consequently, the ecosystem and its surroundings are now home to trees over 100 years old. This conservation initiative has effectively protected the environment and maintained the health of the ecosystem. The community also engages in sustainable farming practices, despite many young residents preferring careers in trade, construction, electrical work, plumbing, solar energy, service industries, and small-scale manufacturing. Moreover, with backing from traditional authorities, these rural organisations have

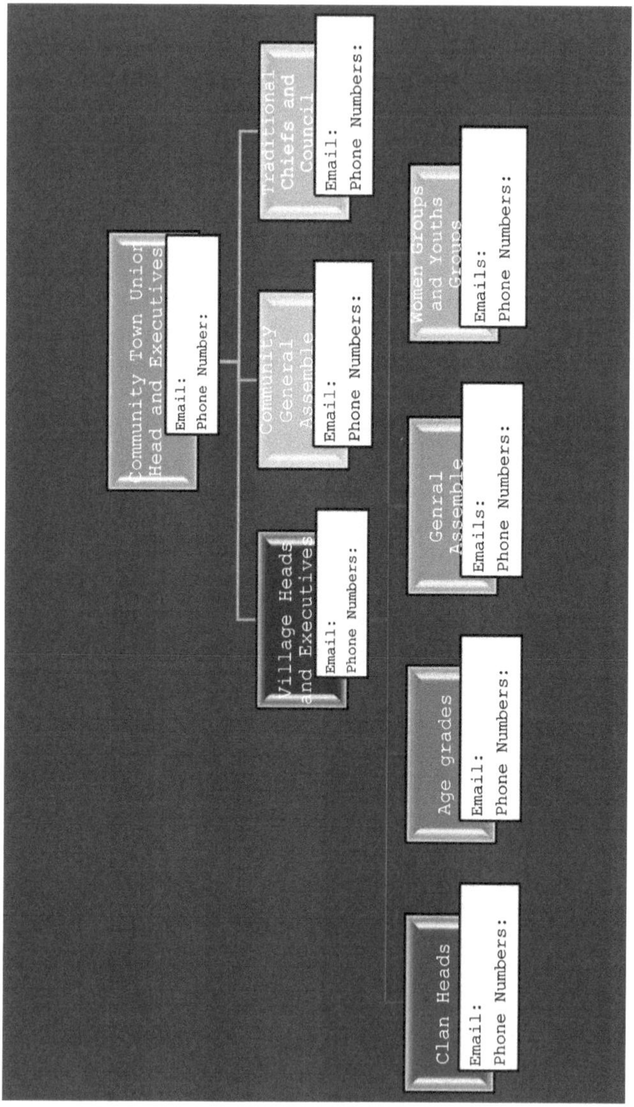

Fig. 8.1 Rural organisation organogram (*Source* Author 2025)

played a vital role in preserving local culture and traditional knowledge, which has boosted tourism and supported social and economic growth.

Rural organisations face challenges such as limited government funding, which is often supplemented by donations from NGOs, community members, or mandatory contributions, thereby restricting the development potential in rural areas. Additional issues include political interference, which can lead to confusion during project initiation and planning, as well as limited leadership capacity. Government support could help overcome these obstacles through effective policies, leadership training, and leveraging technological innovations. Rural organisations are vital for driving economic change and supporting livelihood strategies in rural communities. Success depends heavily on community involvement and transparency, with a structure that allows community members to hold leaders accountable.

8.3 Local Government or Municipality

Local governments or municipalities are vital for rural development, providing essential services, boosting local economies, and promoting community involvement to improve residents' quality of life. Their organisational structure should include a dedicated "Rural Development" unit, reporting to the Municipal Manager and, ideally, the executive Chairman or Mayor. This unit manages various initiatives, collaborating with funders, state or provincial governments, and national departments like South Africa's Department of Rural Development and Land Reform (DRDLR). It also partners with community-based organisations and private sector stakeholders to address infrastructure, agriculture, skills training, SMMEs, entrepreneurship, and social services in rural areas. This book explores the organisational structures of Nigerian and South African municipalities to evaluate their roles in unlocking rural potential and fostering rural development.

8.3.1 Nigeria Local Governments (Southeastern Nigeria)

This section examines the possible role of local government in rural settlement development by analysing the organisational structure of local government in the Southeastern region. According to the 1999 Nigerian Constitution, a democratically elected local government system is assured, with Section 7(1) requiring state governments to establish a structure and finance local governments through legislation. The functions of local governments, outlined in the Nigerian constitution, include providing economic advice, collecting taxes and fees, and developing and maintaining infrastructure and services. The 1999 constitution established local governments as the third tier of government, implying they are the primary planning authority at the grassroots level. As the closest level of government to the public, local governments are best placed to mobilise citizens and material resources through public involvement, facilitating rapid social and economic growth. They are also well-suited to provide local services and make development activities responsive to local needs and initiatives. Figure 8.2 illustrates a typical Local Government Leadership Organogram in the Southeastern States of Nigeria. However, many rural local governments struggle to perform their functions due to financial constraints and a corrupt system that allows state governments to control their finances.

Figure 8.2 depicts the organisational structure, with the Executive Chairman at the top, elected alongside the Vice-Chairman and Councillors. The legislative branch of the local government comprises elected councillors from various wards within the area. The Executive Chairman and councillors then choose a Leader and Deputy Leader. Subsequently, the Executive Chairman appoints Supervisory Councillors from the ward councillors to oversee specific departments, such as Agriculture, Finance, Health, and Education, ensuring effective service delivery and rural development. Importantly, permanent roles, such as Heads of Departments, are not appointed by the Executive Chairman but are selected through a formal recruitment process. These department heads are responsible for managing daily operations to fulfil the local government's mandate, guided by their vision and objectives.

The 1999 Nigerian constitution provided for financial decentralisation, allowing local governments to be autonomous, deliver services, and provide public goods to the people living in their jurisdiction. However, this constitutional right has not been implemented by local governments due to the corrupt tendencies of political elites and actors at the state level, as well as the lack of federal government monitoring or oversight of local government administration. This has limited the functions of the local government and impacted rural development.

For local governments in rural areas to be practical and functional, they require strong leadership and stable financial support. Local government can gain a good reputation if it provides for the needs of its residents. Kyriacou et al. (2015) believe that the fiscal capability of sub-central governments can promote regional convergence because of the expectation that lower levels of government will respond more efficiently to local needs because they can provide better-informed

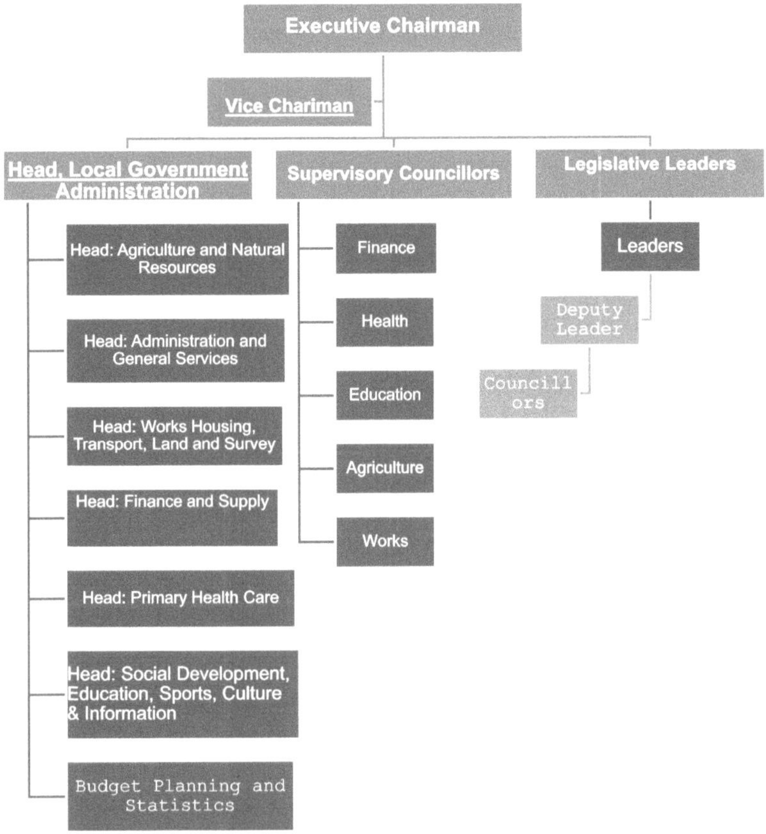

Fig. 8.2 Typical local government organogram in Southeastern Nigeria (*Source* Author 2025)

and tailor-made policies or because they strive to preserve or increase their tax base in the face of competition from other regions. Martinez-Vazquez et al. (2016) stated that fiscal decentralisation at the local governments considerably promotes new economic advancement.

The ineffective decentralisation of power and the erosion of autonomous local government authority have been affected by the federal government allocating money intended for local governments to state governments, believing that the state governments will assist the local governments in implementing their functions. In the true sense, it should help create accountability and effective local government development and service delivery. In reality, it has led to corruption, resulting in local governments suffering a lack of funds to implement projects and administer their day-to-day functions. This is because state governments have failed to reallocate money made for local government roles. Secondly, in many cases, state governments fail to conduct local government elections and instead prefer to appoint administrators who are loyal to them. This creates an avenue for corrupting local government finances, leading to ineffective local governments and a failure to provide services and develop projects.

8.3.2 South Africa Municipality

The South African Constitution includes a concept of "equitable", which relates to national revenue allocation. In Section 227(1) of the Constitution, local governments are entitled to a share of the national government's income. It stipulates that nationally generated income must be distributed fairly among national, provincial, and municipal levels of government. The sharing of income depends on the functions each level of government performs and the revenue it can generate.

It is crucial to note that equitable rural development involves applying fairness norms to foster healthy, vibrant, and sustainable communities in rural areas. Therefore, equitable outcomes should encompass rural development policies and strategies that can be achieved by harnessing rural potential and leveraging rural opportunities to shape their communities. For rural areas to participate in South Africa's shared vision, strategic targets should be established to address disparities between urban and rural areas, including unemployment, poverty, infrastructure, social services, and economic development. Rural areas should have an equal share in promoting social and economic investment that drives private business investment in rural communities. The positive effects of equitable development include transforming poverty-stricken communities into mixed-income communities through diverse social and economic investments, new housing developments, and infrastructure projects. A positive impact of equity fosters social networks and services utilised by communities, supporting the creation of additional viable businesses in rural areas. Some of the roles of municipalities in South Africa include:

1. To ensure that rural areas have access to clean water, sanitation facilities, electricity, and decent housing, which are fundamental for enhancing living standards in rural areas.
2. Initiating, planning, implementing and maintaining rural roads, bridges, and other necessary infrastructure through community participation to enable better networks and smooth economic activities.
3. Encourage and support small businesses and entrepreneurs in rural areas through initiatives such as training, skills development, market access, and facilities like shops and business locations to stimulate economic development, growth, and job creation.
4. Develop a municipal spatial plan and land use plan that supports and guides development in rural areas, maximising their potential by identifying suitable areas for businesses, agricultural development, industrial growth, housing, and other social and economic activities and opportunities.
5. Support communities' participation in all matters and activities that concern the local government and rural development. Ensure that rural communities and populations are involved in decision-making to ensure programme and project priorities.
6. Support the advancement and collaborate with other spheres of government, the private sector, and NGOs to leverage their financial expertise, skills, and investment opportunities for rural development programmes and projects.
7. Establish mechanisms and structures to continuously monitor the potentials and challenges of rural areas for effective rural development initiatives, social and economic improvement, and sustainable development.

Other important aspects of the municipality and local government include ensuring democratic and accountable governance for rural communities, empowering residents to increase income, and stimulating local investment. Local governments should deliver vital services and infrastructure that protect lives, property, and promote a healthy environment, while also supporting skills development and encouraging healthy lifestyles.

Local governments face several challenges in performing their duties effectively. They often have limited financial resources due to a small tax base and insufficient investment to generate revenue and taxes. A key issue for rural local governments is a lack of income, caused by residents not paying for services, corrupt procurement practices, weak accountability measures, and a shortage of institutional capacity and skilled professionals. Additionally, technological development is limited, and there is a lack of data to inform decisions. This situation hampers municipalities' ability to be self-sufficient, creating a dependency cycle on provincial and national support. The dispersed community residential system also raises costs and reduces efficiency in service delivery. Moreover, some local governments struggle to implement plans and programmes, often due to inadequate funds and a lack of skills needed to support their roles.

8.4 State and Provincial Government

State and provincial governments play a crucial role in rural development, managing departments that coordinate projects, allocate resources, promote local economic growth, ensure access to land through tenure and ownership, improve infrastructure, create jobs to reduce unemployment, and provide essential services. Therefore, it is important to evaluate the roles of Nigerian state governments and South African provincial governments in rural development. Although they operate at similar levels—referred to as states in Nigeria and provinces in South Africa—they both serve as the second tier of government, subordinate to the national authorities.

8.4.1 Nigeria State Governments

State governments are responsible for establishing and overseeing local government councils within their respective states, ensuring that these councils have the necessary resources and expertise to serve their communities effectively. In Nigeria, state governments create policies and provide administrative oversight for local governments, which are responsible for rural development. The supposed state's role in rural development can be summarised as follows.

- Create policies that support local governments to deliver their social and economic mandate and activities
- Oversee the quality and quantity of services provided by local governments
- Provide funding to local governments when they lack resources

Nwokwu et al. (2023) state that Section 162(5) of the Nigerian Constitution of 1999 stipulates that the money to be credited to the local government councils in the Federation Account shall be allocated to the states for the benefit of their local government councils, as may be agreed upon by the National Assembly. The constitution further stipulates in subsection six that each state shall create a state joint local government account into which allocations to the local government councils of the state from the federation account shall be paid. Then, Section 7(3) of the 1999 Constitution permits the state houses of assembly to establish an Economic Planning Board to encourage the participation of local governments in the state's economic planning and development, especially in areas of mutual benefit (Nwokwu et al., 2023). The idea is that, given the limited resources of the local governments, the state government would help in jointly financing local government projects and programmes. The ideology is to assist the local government with financial cooperation with the state government, which could lead to rapid and sustainable rural development.

Awkwardly, this financial situation does not help the local governments in Nigeria but retard the social and economic growth of local government due to its limitation and corruption of the many state governors who use the allocated local government money for their own selfish agender. Where the state determines the fate of thc local government, instead of a healthy relationship of equity to enhance rural development. Fatile et al. (2017) stated that many state governments were engaged in superfluous deductions and often diverted funds from the state joint local government account to areas of personal interest, thereby decelerating the pace of development at the local government level, which affects rural development.

For the past two decades, the toothlessness problem in Nigeria's federalism has been the failure to grant fiscal autonomy to local governments as the third tier of government. The local government has been underdeveloped due to the state government's financial control over its resources and the local government's lack of financial autonomy.

The outcome of limited rural development in many parts of Nigeria has led to the migration of youths from rural to urban areas, seeking better opportunities and creating a skills gap in rural areas. In Ahiazu Mbaise, Imo State, Nigeria, the operations of state joint local government accounts have not improved the provision of rural infrastructure. Ahiazu has one of the worst road networks in Imo State. There is no proper sanitation system, and almost all households rely on personal water supplies, which are not suitable for drinking. Some households rely on river water, while others use streams. Communities provide funded electrification of their villages without government assistance through individual contributions and efforts. There are no health facilities; however, a few clinics are financed by the communities.

The consequence of the findings is that if local governments in Imo State are not granted financial autonomy, sustainable development of the rural areas will continue to elude the state and the local government areas. Jutting (2005) indicated that there was no clear relationship between decentralisation and the reduction of poverty; however, the state's failure to provide sufficient financial support to local governments was a hindrance to rural development in Nigeria.

8.4.2 South Africa Provincial Governments

All three spheres of government share a standard constitutional duty to provide basic and other services to the people and communities within their areas of jurisdiction, as outlined in Section 41(1b) of the Constitution. With respect to Chapter 14, Schedule 4, Part A of the RSA Constitution, rural development is classified within the functional areas of concurrent national and provincial legislative competence. At the provincial level, this function falls under the Provincial Departments of Agriculture and Rural Development.

The book explores the role of the Free State Provincial Government in rural development. The Free State Province was selected due to its location and the potential for numerous rural municipalities within it, unlike the Western Cape and Gauteng, which are primarily urban areas. Rural development in the Free State is overseen by the Free State Provincial Department of Agriculture, Rural Development, and Environmental Affairs, which has eight programmes aligned with its rural development mandate.

The Free State Department of Agriculture, Rural Development, and Environment's 8 Programmes aim to promote rural growth. Central to this is empowering communities to lead their development and shape their futures. Additionally, the programme references a study identifying significant challenges faced by rural residents. By addressing these issues, it seeks to curb rural-to-urban migration (FS...). Below is an outline of how Programme 8 approaches rural development challenges.

1. Institutional development: To assist rural populations and communities in setting their priorities through accountable and transparent processes by providing the local capacity and access to funds to plan and implement local economic development.
2. Investment in basic infrastructure and social services: To provide essential infrastructure, such as housing, water, and power supplies, as well as transport and social services, including basic healthcare and education.
3. Improving income and employment opportunities: To enhance access to natural resources, we will assist in developing the potential of rural areas,

including arable and grazing land, irrigation water, woodland, and forests. Also, investing efforts in the sustainable use of natural resources.

4. Restoration of fundamental economic rights to marginalised rural areas: establishing periodic markets as the spatial and temporal framework for development.
5. Justice, equity, and security: to mitigate past injustices and ensure the rural population's safety and security, especially that of women.

To address the issues identified by the Free State Department of Agriculture, Rural Development, and Environmental Affairs in rural areas, the department introduced five strategic plans aimed at transforming and creating sustainable rural development. The strategic plans are to facilitate rural development and social inclusion through a partnership and participatory approach. These approaches are:

1. Institutional Coordination: It promotes "Participatory Rural Appraisal". It adopts a bottom-up approach, involving the community from the outset of any project. The provincial government's idea is to establish a structure called the Council of Stakeholders, which aims to identify local issues and collaborate with communities to develop mechanisms to address them. The suggestion for the members of the Council of Stakeholders is.
   A. Traditional leadership *and or* Ward Councillors
   B. Government Officials (Both Departmental and Municipal officials)
   C. Non-Governmental Organisations
   D. Community-Based Organisations
   E. Faith-Based Organisations
   F. Private sector/Business, etc.

   The Council of Stakeholders identifies all projects or potential projects in the area and then, with the aid of the communities, prioritises them from greatest to least need. The Council of Stakeholders considers the plans already featured or committed in the area's Integrated Development Plan (IDP). This unit is responsible for tracking performance progress in the province.
2. Agrarian Transformation: This programme drives changes in land, livestock, cropping, and community systems by coordinating all provincial rural initiatives. It emphasises, but is not limited to, creating business ventures, agro-industries, cooperatives, cultural projects, and lively local markets. The programme also seeks to empower rural residents and communities, especially women and youth. It aims to revitalise and upgrade economic, social, information, and communication infrastructure, along with public amenities in rural

areas, including villages and small towns. Furthermore, it creates a database of unemployed rural youth who can participate in the National Rural Youth Service Corps (NARYSEC) Programme. The program further coordinates support for restitution farms, agri-villages, and rural initiatives to promote sustainable rural development.

3. Rural Infrastructure Development: It promotes consultation with local government structures and the community to facilitate the provision of rural infrastructure projects as tabled/prioritised during the Council of Stakeholders. The rural infrastructure development programme helps to conduct a project scope assessment, followed by a project scope and, where possible, a project plan. This is achieved through the cooperation of national and provincial line departments, as well as local municipalities, for infrastructural development.
4. Community Mobilisation and Social Organisation: The programme assesses community and household needs through profiling and develops a database of households living in poverty. This helps us identify which government services individuals are eligible for but are not currently accessed, and pinpoint specific government interventions tailored to the needs of particular households and communities. We then coordinate with the relevant implementing agents for follow-up. The programme prioritises mass mobilisation, service delivery, collaboration, and partnerships, using a "Buntu" approach to show that "together, we can achieve more".
5. Rural Livelihood and Food Security: This program collaborates with various initiatives to alleviate food insecurity and promote a healthy living standard in communities and households. It upholds South Africa's constitution, which guarantees the rights of all individuals and affirms democratic values such as human dignity, equality, and freedom (e.g. Section 27: Healthcare, food, water, and social security). The program highlights the following rights that are accessible to everyone.
   A. Health care services, including reproductive health care.
   B. Sufficient food and water; and
   C. Social security, including appropriate social assistance if they cannot support themselves and their dependents.

The programme aims to ensure food availability, access, utilisation, and stability. The team managing the programme works with multiple departments, such as Health, Social Development, Education, and Water Affairs, to improve food production and related facilities, supporting rural development in the province.

8.5 National Governments

The national government is vital to rural development by formulating comprehensive policies and strategies. Additionally, it creates integrated programmes to support the sustainable growth of rural regions. These programmes often involve initiating, coordinating, and facilitating initiatives, increasing land access, promoting sustainable farming practices, and improving rural infrastructure and services. The goal is to foster equitable and sustainable rural communities. Analysing the roles of Nigeria's and South Africa's governments helps understand their contributions to rural development.

8.5.1 South Africa National Government

At the national level, rural development in South Africa is primarily functioned within the Department of Agriculture, Land Reform and Rural Development (DALRRD), which is mandated to develop policy, strategy, legislation, and programmes, and oversee the initiation, planning, implementation, and evaluation of rural development. Through the DALRRD, the national government implements rural development by executing policies to minimise or stop the unique challenges of rural areas, including social facilities, infrastructure, economic diversification, training, skill capacitation, and access to education and healthcare. They promote rural economic development and growth by supporting small-scale enterprises and promoting access to land. These actions aim to improve the livelihoods of rural communities, attract investments, and create opportunities. DALRRD carries out these functions through stakeholder engagement with communities, other government institutions, municipalities, and relevant departments. The DALRRD structure for rural development is shown in Fig. 8.3.

As shown in Fig. 8.3, the Minister of DALRRD is the department's overall head and leads rural development in South Africa. The office is supported by two deputy ministers, with the Director General's office overseeing the 11 units that manage programme initiations, plans, implementation, and evaluation. These 11 programmes enable the smooth rollout of rural development and promote greater transparency and accountability.

The South African government, via the President, introduced the Comprehensive Rural Development Programme (CRDP) in July 2009, serving as the flagship initiative of the Department of Agriculture, Land Reform, and Rural Development. The department primarily aims to drive rural transformation. The CRDP

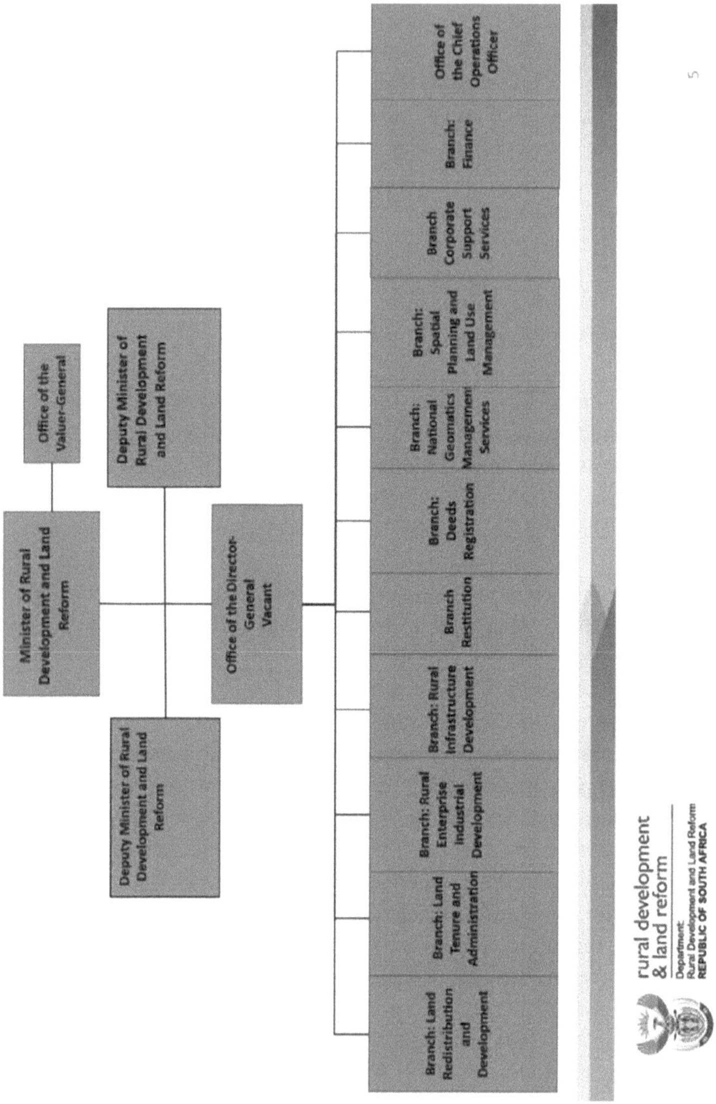

Fig. 8.3 National government rural development structure (*Source* DALRRD (2019))

seeks to coordinate efforts across various government sectors to improve rural areas through integrated development programmes. Its national scope includes three key elements: land reform, agrarian transformation, and rural development. This framework supports the government's rural development goals through DLRRD.

DALRRD (2019) indicated that CRDP is developed through lessons learnt from pilot sites selected based on social and economic profiling, community participatory processes, and intergovernmental cooperation. The primary baseline data were collected from the first two pilot engagements, conducted in Riemvasmaak, Northern Cape, and Muyexe Village, Giyani, Limpopo. According to the CRDP policy paper, the strategic objective is to facilitate integrated development and social cohesion through participatory approaches in partnership with all sectors of society in South Africa through:

1. Contributing to the redistribution of 30% of the country's agricultural land
2. Improving food security of the rural poor
3. Creating business opportunities
4. Decongesting and rehabilitating overcrowded former homeland areas
5. Expanding opportunities for rural women, youth, people with disabilities, and older persons.

An inclusive CRDP stakeholder participation model was created as the Council of Stakeholders, which collaborates as partners in planning, implementation, and monitoring. This approach places communities at the heart of their development process. According to DALRRD, the work carried out at CRDP sites, in partnership with other departments at national, provincial, and local levels, has led to the construction of infrastructure such as housing, water supplies, sanitation, pack-sheds, community halls, multipurpose centres, fencing, early childhood development centres, satellite police stations, and the renovation of schools and clinics.

In 2023, the Department of Agriculture, Land Reform, and Rural Development developed a more comprehensive and inclusive rural development framework, known as the Integrated Rural Development Sector Strategy (IRDSS). The Integrated Rural Development Sector Strategy draws lessons from the successes and weaknesses identified in implementing the Comprehensive Rural Development Programme, which encompasses intergovernmental relations. According to the IRDSS, the objectives of Rural Development (DALRRD 2023, p. 5) are

Rural development seeks to:

1. Address the triple challenges of poverty, inequality, and unemployment in rural areas.
2. Improve the quality of life for rural communities by accelerating the implementation of the National Development Plan and the Economic Reconstruction and Recovery Plan to end poverty and hunger, enhance productivity and food security, and create jobs.
3. Revitalise the rural economy through investment and development of rural infrastructure, including road and transportation, agriculture and agro-processing, mining, digital economy, ocean economy, tourism, arts and culture, water and irrigation schemes, and public health and education.
4. Promote support of rural enterprises and cooperatives to promote self-sustainability and active participation in the economic value chain.
5. Contribute to effective land administration and spatial planning, increasing human settlement, land productivity, and industrialisation.
6. Provide quality education and skills development; and
7. Implement youth and women development and empowerment programmes.

While the objectives of the Integrated Rural Development Sector Strategy are (DALRRD 2023, p. 11).

1. Provide a guiding framework and principles for executing the government's vision, plans, and budget relating to rural development and the revitalisation of the rural economy through the Comprehensive Rural Development Programme and Rural Development Sector Plans.
2. Effective utilisation of all funding instruments across all spheres of government to foster an integrated approach to revitalising rural areas.
3. Institutionalise rural development and strengthen intergovernmental sector coordination through the District Development Model (One Plan) with precise monitoring and reporting systems. Compel all sector departments in all spheres to share their plans and budgets for implementation through the DDM One Plan.
4. Accelerate investment in and maintenance of critical infrastructure, including road, rail, and port essential services, as well as digital connectivity, education, health, and human settlement infrastructure, to revitalise rural economic development and facilitate industrialisation, agricultural production, agro-processing, value chain management, and access to markets.
5. Support integrated spatial planning, land-use management, and economic integration.

The IRDSS objectives will be achieved through the six pillars of the Department of Agriculture, Land Reform and Rural Development (DALRRD). These Pillars are.

Pillar 1: Infrastructure Development, Maintenance, and Investment
Rapid infrastructure development in rural areas broadens access to essential services and boosts the rural economy's competitiveness. It facilitates integrated infrastructure projects aimed at transforming the rural economy, encouraging productive land use, generating employment, and fostering entrepreneurship through improvements in social and economic public infrastructure. These initiatives are designed to connect rural infrastructure with national systems, improving market access and driving social and economic growth in rural communities.

It supports the enhancement and development of infrastructure that promotes mining areas, agricultural production, agro-processing, housing, and water and irrigation systems. Additionally, it helps in constructing schools that foster skill development and reduce illiteracy. Meanwhile, investments in roads, energy, transportation networks, railroads, and logistics will boost rural development. The pillar also aims to improve tourism access by making it easier and better to reach tourism sites. The pillar also supports improving access to mobile networks and the internet, reducing costs, and enhancing rural production's access to regional and global value chains. Pillar 1 is also anchored in a sustainable environment, climate change, and the rehabilitation and restoration of Wetlands to ensure sustainable rural development and encourage conservation that can lead to ecotourism and other economic activities while maintaining balanced ecosystems.

Pillar 2: Industrialisation, Enterprise Development, and Job Creation
The programme aims to support strategies, such as the National Integrated Small Enterprise Development (NISED) Masterplan, to strengthen existing youth initiatives. These initiatives include the National Rural Youth Service Corps Programme, Harambee Youth Employment Accelerator, National Youth Service Programme, and other youth programmes nationwide, through collaborations with youth structures. To bolster the NISED, the Department of Small Business Development has launched the Township and Rural Entrepreneurship Programme (TREP), a dedicated initiative focused on transforming and integrating opportunities in townships and rural areas into productive business ventures. Rural small and medium enterprises (SMMEs) and cooperatives should be incorporated into the economic value chains.

Pillar 3: Education and Skills Development

The programme supports investment in human capital, such as skills, technological expertise, and institutional capacities, which is vital for sustainable rural development. Since the government prioritises rural progress, the skills development system must better focus on industry-relevant skills crucial for both rural growth and the broader rural economy. This approach distinguishes between simply training rural populations and developing skills specifically for rural development. Instead of training rural residents as a means for urban migration, education and skills enhancement should aim to improve rural competencies and education to support the local economy.

Pillar 4: Provision of Basic Services

DALRRD supports Chapter 6 of the National Development Plan by providing essential quality services such as education, water and sanitation, electricity, healthcare, public transport, and roads. These services help build and sustain functional communities that engage actively in social and economic activities. Furthermore, local governments strive to deliver these vital services to all households within their areas, including those in main towns, small towns, villages, farms, and rural regions.

Pillar 5: Land and Agrarian Reform and Tenure Security

Chapter 6 of the National Development Plan highlights that an effective rural development strategy should prioritise agricultural development, rooted in successful land reform, job creation, and environmental sustainability. To achieve this, it acknowledges the need to increase agricultural production and agro-processing, with a focus on smallholder farmers where possible. The pillar highlights that the current economic conditions in communal areas are primarily due to unresolved land tenure rights, unclear communal boundaries, and issues related to land administration, which the government must address through suitable regulatory and policy frameworks.

Pillar 6: Social, Community, and Human Development

This pillar empowers rural communities to actively participate in planning and executing rural development projects, crucial for sustainable progress. It emphasises stakeholder engagement and encourages community involvement in development efforts. DALRRD states that this can be facilitated through participatory processes within existing structures like ward committees and district councils. Additionally, community-based plans should be integrated into RDSPs and IDPs to strengthen support for these initiatives.

The above pillars will yield the desired results if active rural community participation expands the abilities and support of households, the basic units of production, and ensures inclusive and participatory decision-making processes. It could be done according to DALRRD (2023) through the following:

1. Community mobilisation for social action, social cohesion, and as part of skills development for communities, civil society organisations, families, households, and individuals.
2. Community dialogues to identify assets and potential, and to develop community plans.
3. Development of community-based plans to drive potential poverty alleviation projects.
4. Implement social sector programmes to provide specialised social services such as school nutrition, mass literacy, victim empowerment, and community-based care.

DALRRD has urged sectoral departments within the social security cluster to collaborate and foster social cohesion and nation-building, which will contribute to rural development. By leveraging arts and culture, they can utilise various artistic expressions such as music, poetry, and theatre to stimulate rural progress, enhance social cohesion, and support economic growth. Creating rural sports facilities and programmes can increase community participation, promote wellness, and strengthen social bonds, aligning with sectors like health, education, the economy, and social upliftment. DALRRD also advocates for the Department of Basic Education and the Department of Sports, Arts, and Culture to reintroduce sports in schools jointly.

8.5.2 Nigeria National Government

The NNDP (2021, p. 50), the Nigeria National Development Plan, states that "approximately half of Nigeria's population lives in rural areas. 52% of the rural population is classified as poor." The policy document further indicated that agriculture is the primary driver of economic activity in rural areas, contributing to 90% of the food produced in Nigeria. Despite this, the NNDP (2021) states that weak infrastructure, limited processing capabilities, and insufficient packaging result in waste of up to 20% to 60% of the produced food. Therefore, to reduce poverty and stimulate economic growth, it is essential to create an inclusive rural development plan that provides infrastructure in rural areas, thereby encouraging investment in agriculture and related economic activities. To implement the Nigerian National Development Plan (NNDP) strategy for rural development, "Integrated Rural Development" was developed in Chapter 5, on page 50, with the following objectives.

1. Minimise disparities in access to public services between rural and urban areas nationwide
2. Increase rural transportation infrastructure
3. Minimise disparity in economic development between rural and urban areas nationwide

To realise the objectives of rural development across the six geopolitical zones (Southeast, South-South, Southwest, Northwest, Northeast, and North-Central) and to open opportunities for rural areas, ensuring balanced development and increased competitiveness, the NNDP (2021) outlines the following strategies.

1. To increase national agricultural productivity and reduce post-harvest losses in rural areas where agricultural production takes place.
2. To use production systems and technology to increase agricultural output and productivity for priority crop value chains such as cassava, rice, maize, soybean, yam, and tomatoes.
3. To strengthen institutions such as the Nigerian Agricultural Insurance Corporation (NAIC) to increase insurance coverage for floods and post-harvest losses that farmers suffer.
4. To strengthen existing legislation enacted for commodity exchange operations, warehousing, and trading of produce.
5. The administration and capacity of silo complexes at Lafia, Minna, Gusau, Dutsinma, Yola, Akure, and Ilesha, as well as the National Reserve mechanism, will be revamped to ensure efficiency, effectiveness, and transparency.
6. To reduce post-harvest losses, the government will prioritise developing critical rural infrastructure such as roads, reactivation of grain aggregation centres, off-grid energy solutions, and ICT.
7. Increase livestock and aquaculture productivity by implementing the National Livestock Transformation Plan targeted at animal breeding and conservation, grazing reserves development, dairy value chain development, and small ruminant development; the National Accelerated Fish Production Programme and enforce the National Dairy Policy.

8. The government should eliminate the smuggling of fish and poultry to curb illegal fishing and promote the development of the blue economy. The government should address related issues, such as pest and disease control, upgrading abattoirs and slaughterhouses, and establishing veterinary services.
9. Strengthen value chain linkages by promoting local sourcing and value addition. These linkages will be fostered to help strengthen the overall industry and create jobs. Additionally, there will be an increased focus on local processing and value addition to ensure the year-round availability and affordability of food.
10. To strengthen the agriculture research institutions with appropriate frameworks for the commercialisation of their research findings and products.
11. Providing sustainable agricultural credit to farmers to improve production, ensuring that women and youth-owned agro-businesses are included in the credit support systems. This will be achieved through partnerships with microfinance institutions, commercial banks, the Bank of Agriculture, and the National Agricultural Insurance Corporation, as well as credit programmes, including the Anchor Borrowers' Programme. Furthermore, it will increase access to credit and other economic opportunities available to micro-enterprises in rural areas, ensuring that rural integration is not limited to agricultural activities. This will enhance non-farm incomes, promote employment generation, and contribute to poverty reduction among the rural population.
12. To enhance security in Nigeria's agricultural investments, develop a policy that supports community policing and empowers farming clusters and associations to ensure safety in their communities.
13. To ensure equity, capacity building, and the inclusion of women and young people in agriculture and food production, the government will draw on the National Agricultural Gender Policy, developed by the Federal Ministry of Agriculture and Rural Development. It will also utilise the National Gender Plan, created by the Federal Ministry of Women Affairs, and existing youth initiatives from the Federal Ministry of Youths and Social Development, the Federal Ministry of Agriculture and Rural Development, and the Federal Ministry of Employment, Labour, and Productivity, as well as similar agencies at the subnational level, to promote the inclusion of women and young people in the agricultural sector.
14. Attain export competitiveness in high-value and priority agricultural products. The government should strengthen the Nigerian Export Promotion Council's ability to facilitate market linkages to private sector exporters via targeted research, leveraging embassies and trade missions.

15. The government will automate the export process for Nigerian food products to ensure transparency and accountability at ports, with a dedicated window for agricultural goods. This will be achieved by collaborating with the Nigerian Export Promotion Council and training institutions to provide targeted export training and capacity building through commodity associations, with a focus on establishing and maintaining standards. Additionally, partnerships with financial service providers will raise awareness of funding opportunities for exporters, develop bespoke financing instruments, and provide incentives for repatriating export sales proceeds.
16. Nigerian embassies and high commissions will have a trading desk and clear targets to support Nigerian exports.
17. To develop critical rural infrastructure, including roads, off-grid energy, and ICT facilities, to initiate rural economic revitalisation. The ideology is to support the emergence of other economic sectors such as light manufacturing, solid minerals, and outsourced services. This is to be achieved through strategies outlined in the National Development Plan 2021–2025, with a focus on energy and transportation, particularly in rural areas. Leverage the National Integrated Infrastructure Master Plan 2015–2048 and the National Renewable Energy Action Plan 2015–2030.
18. Facilitate partnerships between the private and public sectors to accelerate the provision of infrastructure in rural areas. This aims to benefit from economies of scale and enhance the appeal of these investments.
19. The government should invest in and support increased access to quality education and healthcare in rural areas. This initiative will be implemented through education and skills systems that are linked to the comparative potentials and strengths of rural communities, ensuring the alignment of skills and opportunities. Across rural communities, federal, state, and local governments will facilitate private sector innovations in establishing quality and affordable health centres, schools, and skills development centres to enhance the living conditions of rural populations.
20. Adopt an inclusive strategy that improves the social, economic, and environmental sustainability of host mining communities. Furthermore, develop an Artisanal and Small-Scale Mining (ASM) policy as part of a comprehensive rural development strategy that aligns with development plans at all levels of government and connects with other national rural sector strategies.
21. Extend Universal Healthcare Coverage to over half of Nigeria's population in rural and urban areas.
22. Partnering with the Expanded Water Supply, Sanitation and Hygiene (PEWASH) programme aims to achieve universal access to safe drinking

water and adequate sanitation in rural areas. The Federal Ministry of Water Resources will work closely with state and local government authorities responsible for operating and maintaining rural water supply and sanitation schemes, in collaboration with the communities that benefit from them.

The structures and roles of governments in Nigeria and South Africa differ significantly. The levels of government in South Africa have well-developed policies that are integrated across the different spheres and tiers of government. The South African National Development Plan, along with other national rural development policies and programmes, has been incorporated into nearly all provincial and local government policies. Either through their municipalities' IDPs, local economic development, housing settlement developments, agricultural sector plans, and others, these policies align with the South African National Development Plan and other rural development policies and programmes. What it means is quite interesting, as it helps streamline rural development among all the spheres of the government. However, the implementation efficiencies could be challenged due to the high unemployment rate in rural areas, but it is a well-integrated policy and strategy.

In the Nigerian context, the Nigerian National Development Plan is an isolated plan, as no state or local government has developed policies or strategies aligned with the NNDP. It is particularly worrying, especially since NNDP is due to end in 2025, having been in operation for up to four years. This is partly why rural development faces limitations that hold back national economic growth. Moreover, the Federal Ministry of Rural Development lacks a comprehensive policy on rural development that aligns with the National Development Policies or programmes directly related to rural development.

Consequently, states and local governments need to make sure their rural development policies, strategies, and programmes are aligned with the national rural development plan's objectives. These should be created transparently and responsibly, fostering local governments and communities to lead the implementation process.

9 Summary of the Findings

Abstract

The chapter reviews the findings from previous chapters, highlighting social and economic activities that could promote rural development. These include rich natural resources like agriculture, renewable energy, mining, crafts, biodiversity, forestry, and tourism, as well as functioning rural markets and a large youth population that can be mobilised as drivers of development. However, it emphasises that inadequate infrastructure, weak policies, and poor service delivery continue to hinder sustainable growth in rural areas. The chapter also notes that Africa faces several challenges: poor infrastructure such as bad roads, lack of electricity, clean water, and sanitation; limited access to education and healthcare; a digital divide with low internet and mobile access that hampers marketing, communication, and innovation; insufficient funding and banking facilities, including a shortage of credit, government grants, and effective funding strategies; and policy gaps, as many rural governments lack comprehensive economic development plans or effective strategies. When these plans exist, they are often not sustainable or poorly executed. This chapter utilises SWOT analysis (Strengths, Weaknesses, Opportunities, Threats) to summarise rural conditions. It concludes that urgent, inclusive, and holistic rural development plans are essential, emphasising infrastructure, healthcare, education, financial inclusion, and social protection. Policy frameworks should be strategically designed using SWOT to align goals, resources, and opportunities. The chapter also highlights that rural transformation relies on empowering communities, tackling poverty, and mobilising youth and natural resources into productive economic activities.

C. Osuigwe, *Economic Development of Rural Areas*, Sustainable Development Goals Series, https://doi.org/10.1007/978-3-032-10572-1_9

9.1 Introduction

This book examines how rural areas can promote development by enhancing social and economic activities, resulting in improved livelihoods, increased job opportunities, economic empowerment, and vibrant, thriving rural communities. It also examines the challenges and risks facing rural development that influence sustainable rural growth. These efforts aim to foster smart rural communities. The chapter summarises the main findings of the book and offers recommendations in Chapter 10. It employs strategic modelling to realise rural potential and deliver services that support sustainable development in African countries. The book reviews existing literature through rural development frameworks, clarifying key concepts. It also explores case studies from developed, developing, transitional, and African nations, highlighting the dynamics of rural areas along with the strategic plans and policies involved.

Notwithstanding the potential of rural areas in Africa, sustainable social and economic development seems to elude rural communities due to numerous challenges, particularly inadequate infrastructure and poor social service delivery. Moreover, rural areas often suffer from underdeveloped infrastructure, lacking essential amenities such as good roads, clean drinking water, sanitation, and electricity. These limitations hold back the sustainable growth of rural areas. Furthermore, many rural areas lack access to quality education and healthcare. People often have to travel over 50 kilometres to reach healthcare services and higher education, such as colleges and universities. These challenges harm the potential for economic development and growth in rural areas.

Furthermore, limited internet and mobile phone access in many rural areas present significant development challenges and hinder vital marketing and communication efforts necessary for sustainable growth. Without these connections, rural advancement stalls. Mobile phones and the internet facilitate innovative social and economic activities, promoting lively development. In regions lacking these resources, rural growth is often impossible or unsustainable.

Similarly, limited funding and inadequate banking facilities restrict rural areas from reaching their potential. The funding shortage includes limited credit options, a lack of government grants and support, and underdeveloped funding policies and strategies. These issues affect rural areas' ability to achieve social and economic growth.

In evaluating the physical expectations of rural areas, the findings highlight the weaknesses in many African rural development policies and legislative frameworks at the national, state/provincial, and local levels. Numerous local governments in Africa's rural areas lack local economic development plans to address social and economic challenges and outline strategies for rural development. The absence of these policies and strategies hampers participation and stakeholder engagement, thereby stunting rural economies and obstructing sustainable rural development. The book revealed that where local government strategies do exist, they are not comprehensive enough to address the need to leverage the potential for development in rural areas.

Despite these challenges, rural areas are rich in potential, including natural resources that can drive investments in tourism, mining, agricultural development, commercialisation, manufacturing, marine development, agro-processing, and many other sectors. Many rural communities have a well-developed market system, for example, in the eastern part of Nigeria and many parts of West Africa, which could be developed into regional and global value chains. Chapter 7 highlights the importance of rural areas and showcases the potential for developing agriculture, renewable energy, beverages, small-scale mining, forestry management, labour biodiversity, ecotourism, and local crafts, leveraging the vast land and natural resources available in these areas. These potentials can be planned and developed for job creation, improved livelihood standards, and sustainable economic development and growth when reinforced with good and quality infrastructure, access to quality education, healthcare, and market access.

This book utilises SWOT (Strengths, Weaknesses, Opportunities, and Threats) analysis for rural areas, guiding the development of goals, objectives, and strategic frameworks for sustainable rural development. These strategies aim to foster smart communities and villages. The SWOT approach assesses how to develop rural policies, strategic plans, infrastructure, resources, and facilities to promote growth, revitalise the economy, attract investments, and generate employment, thereby supporting Africa's economic progress.

9.2 Rural Development Strengths, Weaknesses, Opportunities, and Threats (SWOT) Analysis

SWOT analysis is a systematic tool used to assess programmes, projects, and institutions, highlighting their strengths, weaknesses, opportunities, and threats. By using SWOT analysis, organisations can work towards achieving their goals and objectives. Identifying a project's weaknesses helps mitigate threats, while capitalising on strengths, overcoming weaknesses, exploring opportunities, and countering threats. According to Coman and Ronen (2009), evaluating strengths and weaknesses can be improved by pinpointing core problems and conducting core competence analysis. Helms and Nixon (2010) noted that SWOT analysis is used to scrutinise strategic management tools, and the book applied it to evaluate the strengths, weaknesses, opportunities, and threats in building a strategic model for leveraging the potential of rural areas, infrastructure, social facilities, and innovative approaches. The following sections provide a more detailed examination of the SWOT analysis.

Strengths, weaknesses, opportunities and threats (SWOT) analysis

Strengths	*Weakness*
1. The policy is evident in the role of rural development in South Africa, but less evident in Nigeria and many other African Countries. There is a lack of alignment in many local governments in implementing rural development policies 2. Factors that encourage companies to invest in rural areas depend on the overall management and infrastructural development of these areas. Some rural areas have comparative advantages for infrastructure that could attract investment, but need better policies and strategies 3. Many national development plans provide good direction for investment and infrastructure to encourage rural development 4. African countries offer an abundant unskilled workforce for rural development 5. Rural areas have the most abundant land for development and investment. What it needs is proper policy, strategies and implementation of rural development plans 6. Spatial Planning is advantageous and organic; rural areas can be efficiently planned to meet the needs of rural development 7. Rural areas have the potential to integrate Africa into international and regional markets, as well as regional and global value chains 8. The available land uses and natural resources have the potential to integrate Africa 9. Indigenous knowledge on culture and biodiversity is a tool for environmental protection and conservation that could create jobs and encourage sustainable development	1. African countries lack an integrated regional system that promotes rural development. African countries have developed rural development plans that are often unrelated to the African Union's Rural Development Plans and strategies 2. Many African countries lack integrated rural development plans that span from national to local government levels 3. Many of the African countries' national Development Plans do not explain how to integrate rural development into local and regional development 4. Innovation-oriented ideas often emerge slowly in rural development plans and initiatives. There are more bureaucratic relationships in rural development than in creating a successful, sustainable rural development 5. Research and Development (R&D) institutions, in collaboration with governments, often lack a focus on rural development, which affects innovation, training, and overall success 6. Lack of rural development logistic hubs 7. Bulk Infrastructure development is severely lacking in rural areas, thereby negatively impacting rural development 8. The social and economic challenges, including unemployment, poverty, and a lack of investment, have a significant impact on rural development in Africa 9. The lack of skilled labour for rural development, resulting from rural-to-urban migration, negatively impacts rural development 10. Many States, provinces, and local governments in Africa lack strategic plans for rural development
Opportunities	*Threats*

(continued)

(continued)

1. Rural development is a tool for strengthening regional and country economic and social development, integration, and growth 2. Rural development presents an opportunity for inclusive social and economic development through increased participation of rural people 3. Rural areas' locations are strategic for economic development investments, as urban areas seem to be congested 4. Many rural areas have access to infrastructure, internet, and mobile networks 5. Many rural areas have semi-developed social and economic nodes that could be expanded for rural development 6. Many rural areas have the potential to serve as Dry Ports and Agricultural Processing Zones because many of them are located within good logistic networks 7. Many rural areas are located along rivers and oceans and serve as opportunities for marine economic rural development and ecotourism activities 8. Rural areas have the potential to support Research and Development (R&D) to encourage social and economic development of rural areas 9. Rural areas have the potential to develop existing cultural, indigenous knowledge, biodiversity, traditional, and craft resources for rural tourism, social and economic development and growth 10. The natural resources abundant in rural areas are sufficient for mining and tourism	1. Rural infrastructure is insufficient to attract investments and promote sustainable development 2. There is limited innovation in promoting high-tech in rural areas due to inadequate infrastructure and limited resources. Upgrading or encouraging innovations will lead to social and economic development and growth in rural areas 3. Limited access to monetary resources in rural areas of Africa poses a threat to rural development plans. More efficient and effective policies and strategies would be the solution for the financial resources 4. The bureaucracy within Africa is one factor that limits the faster and more sustainable development of rural areas. The threat might be related to a limited skilled workforce and policy development 5. The lack of cooperation among government spheres and community involvement in many parts of Africa for rural development initiatives and plans poses a significant threat to sustainable rural development, hindering economic growth and development 6. Poor and limited housing and property development challenge skilled workers who want to relocate to rural areas for opportunities

Source Author (2025)

has guided the strategic approach outlined in this book. Strategic modelling involves providing recommendations through a strategic framework. Below is an outline of the need for a comprehensive rural development plan, including the creation of effective policies and strategies.

1. Since the COVID-19 crisis, African population growth has outpaced real GDP growth, resulting in a decline in living standards in many African countries and creating hardships that have exacerbated social and economic problems.

2. Many African countries are experiencing social and economic challenges; some have entered economic recession, and even countries with positive economic growth are highly challenged by rural poverty. This creates the need for proper rural development planning that is inclusive and sustainable.
3. More than 50% of the African population comprises youths, and the population is continuing to grow. There is an urgent need to plan for the rural development potential and provide the necessary resources to ignite social and economic activities in rural areas. Furthermore, there is a need to harness the potential of this youthful continent, where many reside in rural areas, for economic development and growth.
4. According to the World Bank (2024), since the early 2010s, progress in reducing global extreme poverty has depended more on reducing poverty in Sub-Saharan Africa than it did previously. It further highlighted that even though the extreme poverty rate in Sub-Saharan Africa has fallen over the past three decades, it was at a slower rate than in other continents. The number of people living in extreme poverty in the region has come close to doubling from 282 million in 1990 to 464 million (World Bank, 2024). In 2024, Sub-Saharan Africa accounted for 16 per cent of the world's population, 67 per cent of the people living in extreme poverty, and two-thirds of the world's extremely poor lived in Sub-Saharan Africa (World Bank, 2024). These impoverished people live in the rural areas of Africa.

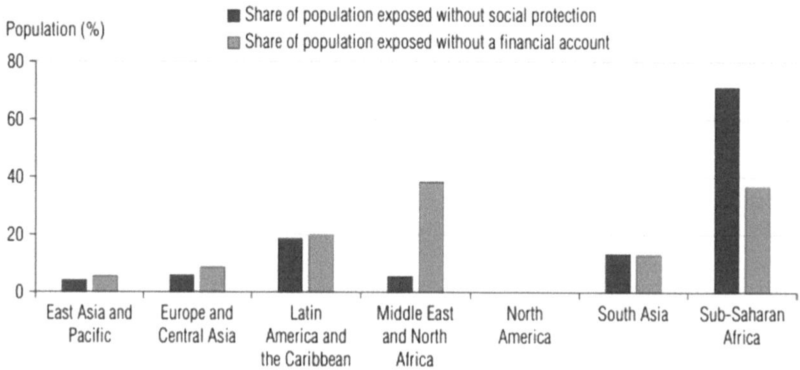

Fig. 9.1 Social protection comparison (*Source* World Bank (2024))

5. Many African countries live with multidimensional poverty, and in 2018/2019, it was stated that almost half (47.3 per cent) of Nigerians were multidimensionally poor.
6. Many African countries lack social protection against emergency periods, old age, unemployment, and for vulnerable individuals. This is clearly shown in Fig. 9.1. The World Bank (2024) states that a large share of the population in Sub-Saharan Africa lacks access to social protection or a financial account.
7. There is poor infrastructural development and limited access to essential social facilities, including education and healthcare, in rural areas.
8. Illiteracy and health challenges are more prominent in rural areas of Africa.

These necessitate the importance of planning an inclusive and holistic strategic rural development plan, as structured in the next chapter.

Chapter Rural Development Strategic Model 10

Abstract

This chapter provides strategic modelling that will assist rural development actors in developing sustainable social and economic development and growth. It focuses on rural development strategies, emphasising the importance of sustainable development for economic, social, and environmental well-being. It highlights the need for comprehensive approaches to tackle rural poverty and outlines a strategic framework for rural development. This framework encompasses multiple sectors, including economic development, infrastructure implementation, human resource development, sustainable land management, community participation, and targeted interventions. The document also discusses the roles of different stakeholders, including governments at various levels, the private sector, NGOs, and local communities, in achieving rural development goals. It emphasises the importance of partnerships and collaboration among these stakeholders to ensure the successful implementation of rural development initiatives. Additionally, it outlines specific programmes and projects aimed at improving agricultural production, environmental sustainability, social planning, and community engagement. It also provides strategic objectives and plans for implementation, along with the partners involved and the support for the United Nations' Sustainable Development Goals.

10.1 Introduction

Developing rural areas sustainably is essential for the economic, social, and environmental well-being of nations. It is just as crucial for reducing poverty, as the vast majority of people living in poverty worldwide are in rural areas (UN, 2020).

C. Osuigwe, *Economic Development of Rural Areas*, Sustainable Development Goals Series, https://doi.org/10.1007/978-3-032-10572-1_10

The evidence shows that national and global targets for poverty reduction will not be met unless rural poverty is tackled. Africa's strategic importance and vast potential as a global source of natural resources cannot be overstated. Nevertheless, the continent faces significant challenges in rural development and has a high level of rural poverty. As a result, there is an urgent need for Africa to adopt more effective approaches to rural development and sustainable economic growth. The rural development recommendation approach is a comprehensive strategic framework for rural development that encompasses social and economic development, infrastructure implementation, human resource development, sustainable land management, community participation, and targeted interventions. This strategic framework will address rural poverty, food security, social and economic investment, and access to basic services, while fostering strong partnerships among the government, private sector, NGOs, and local communities.

According to Osuigwe (2011), someone who correctly identifies the most rational course of action but fails to take it deviates from the power of reason. Rationality involves a leader's or individual's ability to explain their reasoning and actions, using their judgement to justify what they do and demonstrate its suitability (Osuigwe, 2011). Therefore, rationality means doing the right thing for the right reason. As a result, this strategic framework identifies the most effective approach for rural development and comprehensive national social and economic growth. The rural development plan is illustrated in Fig. 10.1, showing the key sectors and factors used in developing the strategic model.

Figure 10.1 illustrates the various roles of players in rural development, including the government, private sector, NGOs, and communities. The government can be further broken down into various government agencies and institutions, including educational bodies responsible for research and training. Figure 10.1 also outlines the key factors that will lead to comprehensive rural development, revitalising social and economic activities in rural areas. It is recommended that all levels of government, including national, provincial, and local authorities, develop a comprehensive strategic framework that models how to allocate resources and enhance potential for sustainable social and economic growth. This framework should aim to:

1. Social and economic diversification of the rural economy through commerce, industrialisation, and mining.
2. Enhance agricultural, forestry, and marine production, and improve agricultural competitiveness through improved production and processing.
3. Impact on environmental sustainability that will foster economic activities.

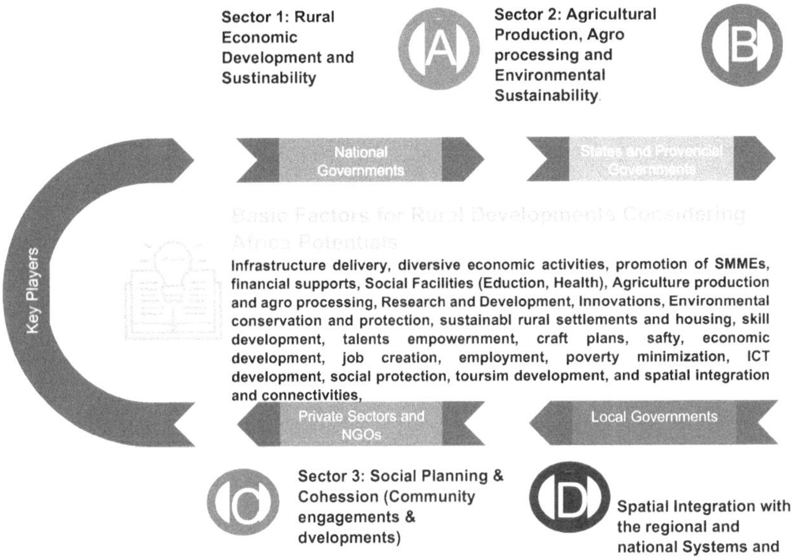

Fig. 10.1 Rural development plan strategic perspective

4. Developing the capacities and skills of a rural area to drive social and economic diversification.
5. Suggest sustainable programmes and projects supporting the United Nations' sustainable development goals.
6. To improve governance, accountability, transparency, and community participation to ensure programme and project sustainability.
7. Develop smart rural settlements or villages that incorporate innovation, technological advancements, green energy, and research.
8. Improve communication systems, IT usage, internet access, and connection to mobile phones to improve market, social cohesion, and rural development.

The rural development strategic framework establishes key objectives and ideas to promote social and economic growth. These objectives are detailed in Table 10.1. Governments at the national, state, provincial, and local levels can modify their rural development plans using this framework. This enables them to leverage the distinct rural potential of their regions and address specific rural challenges effectively.

Table 10.1 Strategic Framework

Strategic Objectives	Plans (programmes and Projects) for Implementation	Partners	Sustainable Development Goal Support
Programme: Agricultural, Fishing, and Forestry			
Human Resources and knowledge development	Build new schools. Build colleges and Higher institutions in rural areas	Communities, UN, World Bank, Governments, Private Sector, and NGOs	Goal 1: No Poverty Goal 2: Zero Hunger Goal 4: Quality Education
	Training of farmers on new techniques and innovations		
	Rehabilitation of schools and delivering quality education through adequately skilled staff		
	Provide vocational training and educational opportunities		
Innovation and Developing Potentials	Develop a forestry economy	Communities, the UN, the World Bank, Governments, the Private Sector, and NGOs	Goal 9: Innovation, Industry, and Infrastructure
	Develop the marine industry in rural areas closer to rivers and oceans		
	Agricultural innovation and technologies		
	Develop infrastructure that supports the agricultural, fishery, and forestry economy in rural areas		
	Improve the agriculture, marine industry, and forestry production and processing perspective		
Production quality and measures	Meeting national and international production and farming standards to enable international and national marketing	Communities, UN, World Bank, Governments, Private Sector, and NGOs	Goal 9: Innovation, Industry, and Infrastructure

(continued)

Table 10.1 (continued)

Strategic Objectives	Plans (programmes and Projects) for Implementation	Partners	Sustainable Development Goal Support
	Producers, farmers, fishers, and foresters should participate in quality programmes		
	Government provision of advisory and extension services to enable quality production		
Programme: Sustainable Environment			
Sustainable use of natural resources	Use of land in a sustainable manner. Ensure that proper land management programmes are in place and acceptable to the communities. It can differ from one rural area to another	Communities, UN, World Bank, Governments, Private Sector, and NGOs	Goal 1: Poverty Reduction Goal 2: Zero Hunger Goal 11: Sustainable Communities Goal 13: Climate Action Goal 15: Life on Land
	Provide animal welfare payments		
	Where possible, support and encourage agroforestry systems on agricultural land		
	Encourage afforestation of non-agricultural land		
	Restoring natural water and forestry potential for social and economic activities		
	Sustainable conservation and biodiversity to support tourism and eco-balance		
	Support ecosystem protection, which could be developed sustainably through tourism		

(continued)

Table 10.1 (continued)

Strategic Objectives	Plans (programmes and Projects) for Implementation	Partners	Sustainable Development Goal Support
Programme: Economic Diversification and Standard of Living			
Diversification of rural economic activities	Provide sustainable financial assistance to small businesses and SMMEs	Communities, UN, World Bank, Governments, Private Sector, and NGOs	Goal 1: Poverty Reduction Goal 5: Gender Equality Goal 8: Decent Work and Economic Growth Goal 9: Industrial and Innovation Goal 10: Reduce Inequality Goal 17: Partnership for the Goals
	Support cross-border facilities to enable engagement and participation in regional chain marketing		
	Support investment in product storage, packaging, trading equipment, and market information		
	Support the development of youth and women for SMMEs and business development		
	Support for tourism activities		
	Support rural periodic markets and help develop facilities at these locations to enable social and economic activities		
Rural area standard of living	Provide and develop basic services for economic growth	Communities, UN, World Bank, Governments, Private Sector, and NGOs	Goal 3: Good Health and Well-being Goal 4: Quality Education Goal 8: Decent Work and Economic Growth Goal 10: Reduce Inequality
	Provide quality education and healthcare that will enhance skill development and promote good health		
	Support cultural and traditional heritage that will revitalise the rural economy		
	Provide training and information on businesses and opportunities		

(continued)

Table 10.1 (continued)

Strategic Objectives	Plans (programmes and Projects) for Implementation	Partners	Sustainable Development Goal Support
	Assist in encouraging and developing rural crafts to create economic opportunities and promote tourism		
	Provide basic welfare programmes for the poor and vulnerable in the rural areas		
	Develop a strategy for community development		
Programme: Governance, Transparency and Accountability			
Implementing local development strategies	Provide support for competitiveness and fairness through policies and strategies	Communities, UN, Governments, Private Sector, and NGOs	Goal 1: Poverty Reduction Goal 4: Quality Education Goal 11: Sustainable Communities Goal 16: Peace, Justice and Strong Institutions Goal 17: Partnership for the Goals
	Provide resource management and accountability		
	Implementing projects through community support and participation		
	Support and enhance community action groups, skills development, and acquisition		
	Strengthen good governance, transparency, and accountability convergence for rural development		
	Develop comprehensive and holistic legislation, policies, and strategies to achieve rural development goals, ensuring a differentiated approach that considers the unique potential and challenges of each area		

(continued)

Table 10.1 (continued)

Strategic Objectives	Plans (programmes and Projects) for Implementation	Partners	Sustainable Development Goal Support
	Develop a "Stakeholders' Framework" for rural development to ensure effective and efficient rural development initiatives, plans, implementation, and evaluations		
	Develop a capacity and framework for knowledge sharing and exchange that will enhance capacity building in social protection, economic development, and community resilience		
	Develop monitoring and evaluation mechanisms to ensure the sustainability of programmes and projects		
Programme: Inclusivity			
Participation	Develop a Multi-stakeholder Framework Document for rural development that ensures the participation of rural women and youth, as well as other vulnerable groups	Communities, UN, World Bank, Governments, Private Sector, and NGOs	Goal 1: Poverty Reduction Goal 10: Reduce Inequality Goal 11: Sustainable Communities Goal 16: Peace, Justice and Strong Institutions Goal 17: Partnership for the Goals
	Support rural people in identifying initiatives that will lead to sustainable rural development		

(continued)

Table 10.1 (continued)

Strategic Objectives	Plans (programmes and Projects) for Implementation	Partners	Sustainable Development Goal Support
	Develop community participation processes. This must be a part of the Multi-Stakeholders Framework Document		
United Nations Sustainable Development Goals	Create and raise awareness of the United Nations Sustainable Development Goals and their importance for rural areas and economic development. Provide systems and actions that translate SDGs into pragmatic actions		
	Develop programmes linked to improving SDGs through rural development that will lead to capacity building, poverty eradication, job creation, and support for businesses and enterprises, as well as business creation. Also, programmes that help alleviate the suffering of vulnerable people and marginalised communities in rural areas should be developed		
	Support poverty eradication initiatives that encourage knowledge empowerment, innovation, and inclusive development		

(continued)

Table 10.1 (continued)

Strategic Objectives	Plans (programmes and Projects) for Implementation	Partners	Sustainable Development Goal Support
Programme: Infrastructure			
Plans and Development	Identification of necessary infrastructural development that is potentially for rural developments, such as electricity, roads, and water	Communities, UN, World Bank, Governments, Private Sector, and NGOs	Goal 1: Poverty Reduction Goal 6: Clean Water Goal 8: Decent Work and Economic Growth Goal 9: Industry and Infrastructure Goal 11: Sustainable Communities Goal 17: Partnership for the Goals
	Empowering rural communities through the sustainable development of their local infrastructure and indigenous knowledge		
	Provide a framework for private and public participation in rural infrastructure development that is cost-effective and leads to rural social and economic activities		
	Provide means of infrastructural finance and investment for receptive small-scale infrastructure developments		
	Develop infrastructure that increases agricultural, forestry, and fisheries production, such as irrigation systems and other production or storage facilities		

(continued)

Table 10.1 (continued)

Strategic Objectives	Plans (programmes and Projects) for Implementation	Partners	Sustainable Development Goal Support
	Provide different modes of transportation to reduce the cost of travelling and economic production		
	Develop infrastructure that supports rural production and services, facilitating the cross-border movement of goods and services, and promoting linkages to regional value chains		
Maintenance	Local governments in rural areas should be equipped with resources to support road maintenance and the construction of small access roads, which can facilitate the transportation of agricultural products		
	Develop community programmes for road maintenance and improvements		
Programme: Social Facilities			
Education	Develop programmes that support access to formal vocational education and human resource development	Communities, UN, World Bank, Governments, Private Sector, and NGOs	Goal 1: No Poverty Goal 2: Zero Hunger Goal 3: Good health and well-being Goal 4: Quality Education Goal 6: Clean Water and Sanitation
	Capacitate local government and communities in developing rural plans, strategies, implementation, and evaluation		
	Build colleges and Higher institutions in rural areas		

(continued)

Table 10.1 (continued)

Strategic Objectives	Plans (programmes and Projects) for Implementation	Partners	Sustainable Development Goal Support
	Ensure that primary and secondary school education is easily accessible in rural areas		
	Develop a knowledge-based management technique that supports natural resource management, climate change adaptation, and mitigation		
Health	Ensure effective local health service delivery		
	Build regional hospitals closer to rural areas and make them accessible to rural areas		
	Ensure good sanitation, water facilities, and infrastructure in rural areas that support good health and well-being		
	Build rural clinics where the thresholds are high enough and provide means to access hospitals		
	Investment in health facilities and infrastructure, as well as prioritisation of service development, is needed		
	Provide mobile clinics to sparsely populated rural areas		

(continued)

Table 10.1 (continued)

Strategic Objectives	Plans (programmes and Projects) for Implementation	Partners	Sustainable Development Goal Support
	Provide daily off-site health consultation services to rural areas where hospitals and clinics are unavailable, utilising mobile phones and internet connections		
Programme: Tourism			
Indigenous Knowledge, Infrastructure and Planning	Share information and knowledge on rural Tourism Development and activities	Communities, UN, World Bank, Governments, Private Sector, and NGOs	Goal 1: Poverty Reduction Goal 5: Gender Equality Goal 10: Reduce Inequality Goal 11: Sustainable Communities Goal 13: Climate Action Goal 17: Partnership for the
	Develop a Rural Tourism Development Framework		
	Support Youths and women in the tourism industry		
	Support security and healthy tourism activities in rural areas		
	Support craft development and marketing		
	Support the development of Tourism facilities		
	Develop rural tourism potential locations		

(continued)

Table 10.1 (continued)

Strategic Objectives	Plans (programmes and Projects) for Implementation	Partners	Sustainable Development Goal Support
	Develop a Rural Tourism activity guide		
	Enhancing the rural tourism development model is closely tied to conserving and promoting traditional and cultural values		
Programme: Industries			
Special Agro-Industrial Processing Zones (SAPZ)	Create SAPZs in rural areas to enable the integrated production, processing, and distribution of targeted crops; this will make agriculture more attractive to young people and increase food production and exports	Communities, UN, World Bank, Governments, Private Sector, and NGOs	Goal 1: Poverty Reduction Goal 8: Decent Work and Economic Growth Goal 9: Industry, Innovation and Industry
Industries	Develop a rural industrial development framework		
	Provide access, funding, and grants to the private sector for industrial development in rural areas		
	Integration industrialisation support from African countries on the free movement of capital, goods, and services		
	Linkages of industrial production to regional and global value chains		

(continued)

Table 10.1 (continued)

Strategic Objectives	Plans (programmes and Projects) for Implementation	Partners	Sustainable Development Goal Support
	Support for intra-African trade in industrialisation		
	Provide facilities and infrastructure that will lead to the industrialisation of rural areas		
	Rural areas' agricultural, forestry, and marine production industrialisation is through the private sector and is assisted by government policies, strategies, and capital		
Programme: Smart Rural Communities			
Research, Development, and Innovation Technology	Share experiences in developing models of digital transformation and innovative new rural construction	Communities, UN, World Bank, Governments, Private Sector, and NGOs	Goal 1: Poverty Reduction Goal 3: Good Health and Well-being Goal 4: Quality Education Goal 7: Affordable and Clean Energy Goal 9: Industry, innovation and infrastructure Goal 10: Reduce Inequality Goal 11: Sustainable Communities Goal 13: Climate Action Goal 17: Partnership for the
	Promote Research and Innovation that will assist rural areas in developing agricultural research to improve farming production		
	Support the application of drones, automated tractors, artificial intelligence, robotics, and blockchains		

(continued)

Table 10.1 (continued)

Strategic Objectives	Plans (programmes and Projects) for Implementation	Partners	Sustainable Development Goal Support
	Promote climate-smart farmers and a Bio-Circular Green Economy in support of rural development and poverty eradication		
Alternative Energy	Develop solar farms or wind turbines in rural communities that can power rural households, agricultural production, and businesses		
	Develop irrigation and farming facilities powered by alternative energy, such as solar and wind		
	Develop schools and health facilities that are supported by wind or solar energy		
	Develop water systems powered by alternative energy, such as wind and solar energy		
ICT and Information	Promote internet and mobile phone networks in rural areas to support marketing and communications		
	Support integrated value chains to enhance market access by expanding Internet and mobile network availability. This connection links rural producers to broader markets, allowing them to sell their goods directly to consumers		

(continued)

Table 10.1 (continued)

Strategic Objectives	Plans (programmes and Projects) for Implementation	Partners	Sustainable Development Goal Support
	Provide Wi-Fi services to rural community nodes. Furthermore, promote the development of digital programmes for collaboration and knowledge sharing among rural communities, villages, and populations		
	To share vital health information and awareness campaigns through mobile platforms		
	Remote health consultation with medical specialists for diagnosis and treatment, especially in rural areas with limited healthcare access		
	Promote online teaching opportunities for teachers and trainers in rural communities		
	Provide rural libraries with internet connections and further promote access to educational materials, books, and courses for rural students, bridging the education gap between urban and rural areas		

(continued)

Table 10.1 (continued)

Strategic Objectives	Plans (programmes and Projects) for Implementation	Partners	Sustainable Development Goal Support
	Create mechanisms that allow easy access to information on farming conditions, such as pest management, appropriate crop varieties for higher yields, and proficient agricultural practices		
	Provide dismantling of weather forecasts on planting and harvesting schedules, mitigating risks from extreme weather conditions through mobile phone accessibility in rural areas		
Artificial intelligence (AI)	Provide AI-powered learning in secondary schools. This is because the rapid advancement of AI presents opportunities for revolutionary education, particularly in secondary and high schools, that will support personalised learning and address diverse student needs		
	Integrate AI into secondary and high schools to enhance engagement and personalise learning to improve outcomes		
	Develop policies and strategies to effectively implement AI in education systems		
	Develop tools for training rural students on using AI for research and to improve businesses and marketing		

10.2 Strategic Framework Modelling

As outlined above, the strategic development framework provides a comprehensive and future-oriented approach to advancing rural development in Africa. This primary goal is supported by various programmes and projects that require careful planning and implementation to promote rural growth effectively. However, for these initiatives to succeed and remain sustainable, active implementation and reliable funding sources are essential; without them, the risk of failure increases. Additionally, establishing a strong organisational structure is vital for ensuring long-term rural development.

10.3 Structure for Rural Development

Given the increasing emphasis on creating a realistic and functional organisational structure for rural communities, Fig. 10.2 presents the recommended structure that will best support rural development within a local government or municipality.

A primary motivation for proposing a rural development organisational structure within local governments and municipalities, as shown in Fig. 9.1, is the lack of existing frameworks in many rural regions. Without proper coordination, rural development initiatives often fail to significantly benefit local communities. The absence of a well-defined structure leads to unsustainable projects, with many initiatives unable to achieve their goals. Moreover, entities like co-operative societies, social clubs, NGOs, as well as individuals and groups, frequently launch projects without adequate oversight and coordination from local authorities, resulting in poor implementation. This situation underscores the necessity for a dedicated rural development directorate to ensure efficient project management and successful delivery in these areas.

The aim in creating an organisational structure for rural development is to ensure that projects are developed and monitored efficiently throughout their implementation by various stakeholders, including private companies, community groups, NGOs, co-operatives, social clubs, and local governments. This structure will facilitate the smooth flow of information between all parties involved in rural development. It will also ensure that project initiators meet the necessary standards. By highlighting the role of co-operatives, social clubs, citizens, and communities, the structure will make it clear that they are integral to rural development. The organisational structure aims to establish a clear monitoring hierarchy within the rural development framework. This structure is designed to ensure that programme and project action plans are implemented in an

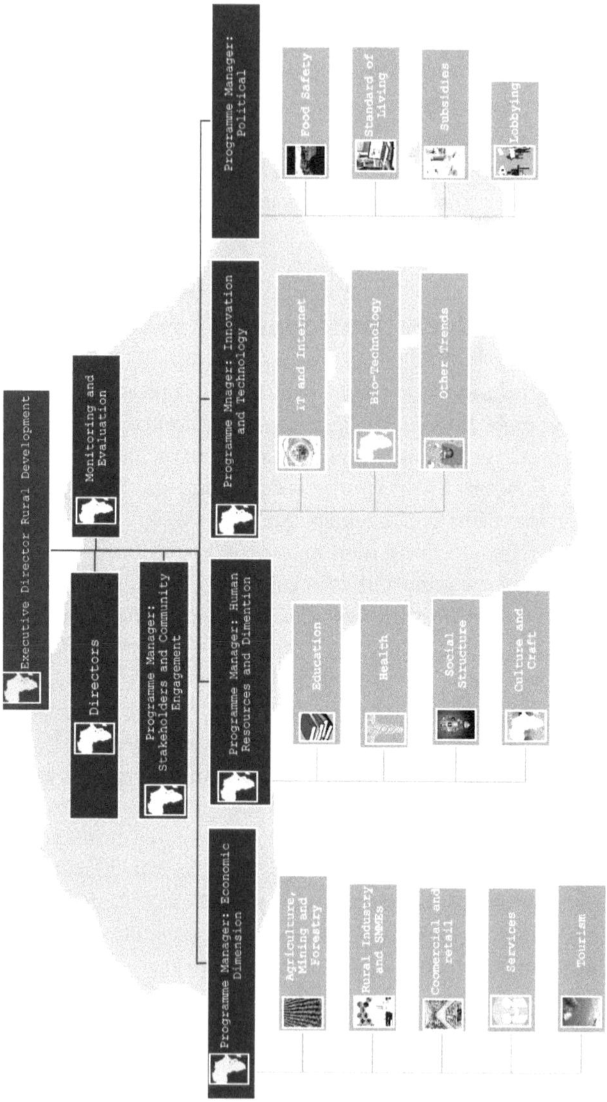

Fig. 10.2 Rural development Organisational Structure (*Source* Author 2025)

accountable and efficient manner, promoting sustainable economic growth and development. The action plans, as identified and examined in Sect. 10.4 below, will be key to achieving this goal.

10.4 Implementation Action Work Plan and Funding for Rural Development

Implementing an action plan helps establish a process to achieve a goal or objective for rural development. This plan includes activities to turn rural policies and strategies into practical, real-world practices. The implementation action process is outlined below.

1. Goals and milestones: Set clear objectives and deliverables with a set of specific, measurable, achievable, relevant, and time-bound goals
2. Risks: Brainstorm and list likely risk, evaluate the risks, and provide mitigation measures to address the risks. Risks can be categorised as low, medium, or high, based on their potential impact. It is advisable to develop a risk matrix. Furthermore, each risk is associated with a stakeholder responsible for mitigating or resolving the risk. The risks should be constantly reviewed to identify further potential risks that could hinder the success of the programme and project, as well as the mitigations that have been provided.
3. Tasks Assignments: Tasks must be delegated to an individual or team member to achieve the desired goal. With task delegation, it would be easy to identify weaknesses and strengths, leading to better programme and project implementations. Assigning tasks gives specific responsibilities to individuals, people, or groups within a programme or project. It could involve allocating tasks to activities to be carried out or assigning tasks during a meeting to achieve a shared goal.
4. Resource Allocations: Allocate capital and tools to complete the programme or projects. It is essential to continually evaluate resources, particularly in Africa, where the prices of materials and services fluctuate due to inflation.
5. Timeframe: Develop a programme plan through the Ghant chart to complete the programme or project. Review the Ghant chant when there are delays, but ensure that the reason for the delays is identified and mitigation measures are provided. Outline the schedule for completing tasks

6. Roles and Responsibilities: Identify the job description and roles of the project team, members, stakeholders, and partners. Ensure that the team, partners, and members responsible sign these project job descriptions and roles to ensure accountability, transparency, and good governance.
7. Communication plan: Develop a programme or project organogram to determine how to communicate with stakeholders and team members. Organograms also help share the information flow, enabling monitoring and taking responsibility. This will allow and enhance easy project implementation and accountability.
8. Budget: Develop a programme or project budget by ensuring that the rural development plan's key needs and priorities are holistically identified. Then, the costs associated with these needs will be identified while exploring potential funding sources to cover them. Break down the revenue streams and expenditure categories based on programme or project phases and development goals.

Building on the action plans, the rural development strategy should bring together a wide range of partners and stakeholders. This approach will foster collaborations among government agencies, private sector entities, NGOs, and community organisations, all working towards sustainable development. It is essential to involve rural communities throughout every phase, from initiation and planning to execution and evaluation. Stakeholders should include women and youth, ensuring their specific needs are met through equal participation. National initiatives should support and align with regional projects and programmes. Partners can collaborate by sharing best practices, highlighting national efforts, organising learning exchanges, and mobilising resources for rural development. Overall, the implementation of the work plan aims to enhance cooperation and advance benefits for Sustainable Development.

Establishment of linkages between community, regional projects, and national initiatives requires stakeholders at the national level to collaborate and execute the work plan. These discussions can address national priority actions, strategies, and coordination mechanisms, fostering effective participation, contribution, and accountability from all involved parties. They also build on the progress achieved during the national consultations that helped develop the work plan.

All levels of government, including national, state/provincial, and local governments, should be responsible for mobilising and managing the resources required to implement the rural development work plan. These include financial and technical resources, as well as other types of support necessary for implementing the work plan and exploring funding mechanisms to ensure the long-term viability of rural development initiatives. It also integrates environmental considerations into all development projects, promoting reforestation, water conservation, and waste management.

Work plans for rural development are established and carried out through budget allocations from national, state, and local governments. Additional funding can also come from regional and international organisations, such as the African Union and its partners, the World Bank, and the United Nations, among others. It is also crucial for stakeholders to provide training and skills development programmes for community leaders, farmers, and other stakeholders to enhance their capacity to manage programmes, projects, and access opportunities. Rural development should be a combined effort, bringing together various initiatives across sectors such as agriculture, education, health, commerce, industrialisation, and infrastructure to create synergy and tackle interconnected issues. A technical programme and project team could be set up at the national and state levels to implement the work plan, tailoring strategies to each rural area's specific needs and conditions. However, a successful implementation action plan requires a well-coordinated stakeholder framework.

10.5 Stakeholders Framework and Participatory Approach

A rural development stakeholders' framework serves as a mechanism to involve various actors—such as policymakers, strategic planners, implementers, interest groups, and beneficiaries—throughout all phases of rural development policies and projects, from planning to implementation, ensuring effective and sustainable outcomes. Implementing rural development projects is complex, partly because it requires satisfying multiple stakeholders. Reed (2008) emphasises that the diverse knowledge and values of rural communities must be incorporated into project execution. According to the United Nations Economic Commission for Europe's 1998 Aarhus Convention, participation in decision-making is a democratic right that supports community involvement in rural development processes. This underpins the stakeholders' framework, because rural development is a cross-sectoral program that demands partnerships with various entities including government, communities, international organisations, the private sector, and NGOs. The framework empowers rural communities to lead development efforts and take ownership of their future.

The stakeholder's framework highlights methods and mechanisms in a programme or project in which stakeholders give their inputs to rural development plans. It also provides processes and methods for stakeholders to direct their concerns and complaints, as well as provide feedback on the programme and project. The main stakeholders in rural development should include the following:

1. Rural community organisations and groups.
2. Rural leadership: Ward Councillors, traditional leaders, and town unions.
3. Rural women's organisations.
4. Rural youth organisations.
5. National, State/Provincial, and Local Governments.
6. Government parastatals and institutions.
7. Academics and researchers.
8. Business organisations, businesspeople operating in rural areas, and the private sector.
9. Programme and project workers.
10. Non-governmental organisations are involved in rural development
11. Members representing people in the government parliaments and legislative assemblies.
12. Media organisation.
13. International organisations such as the World Bank, the Economic Community of West African States, the Southern African Development Community, the United Nations, and the African Union.

The stakeholder framework aims to provide direction and manage stakeholder engagement to meet the standards of practice for our programmes and projects. We achieve this through a range of mechanisms and methods as listed below.

1. Identify the individuals and groups whom the rural development programmes and projects will most influence. These are the affected parties, who are either directly or indirectly impacted by these initiatives. Then, there are the interested parties—individuals, organisations, and groups who have a vested interest in the success or failure of the programmes and projects.
2. Develop a stakeholder organogram to enhance reporting and engagement processes, providing methods that contribute to overall project success.
3. Identify roles, responsibilities, and engagement action plan of each identified stakeholder
4. Develop process meetings and structures to reveal and disseminate programme and project information. The process should provide a mechanism to guarantee regular, accessible, transparent, and accountable consultation.

5. Provide a mechanism for engaging rural communities and populations on the work available in programmes and projects
6. Establish processes for handling complaints and resolving issues.
7. Provide stakeholders with framework reviews and provide mitigation systems.

A successful programme or project signifies an effective participatory method for rural development. Stakeholder participation helps ensure that the programme and project remain relevant and sustainable. It provides a mechanism that facilitates the involvement of marginalised groups and individuals, such as women and vulnerable populations. The participatory approach should encompass the following.

1. Involvement of Beneficiaries: Programmes and projects should involve the project's beneficiaries from initiation to closeout of the programme and project. The beneficiary ideas and expectations should be the primary reason for the programme and projects.
2. Network and Coordination: There should be coordination and a network among stakeholders to facilitate easy participation and ensure the timely delivery of programmes and projects.
3. Good Governance: Participatory monitoring and evaluation should be conducted with an approach that prioritises accountability and transparency for the project's overall success and the benefit of its beneficiaries.
4. Resources and skills: Beneficiaries and stakeholders should have access to the necessary resources, such as funds and skills, to participate effectively in the programme and project activities. The program and project funds could serve as a means to train them in participatory methods, data collection, and analysis, which can contribute to the overall success of the project.
5. Strategic Participatory: Participatory mechanisms can be strategic in context, alongside social and economic factors. This would enable easy management and a faster way for stakeholders to provide results and address challenges.

Effective programmes and mechanisms for project participation are vital for ensuring impactful and sustainable outcomes. Achieving this requires involving beneficiaries, equipping them with the necessary skills and resources, coordinating stakeholders efficiently, and maintaining accountability and transparency in networking and project processes.

10.6 Monitoring and Evaluation

Rural development programmes and projects utilise monitoring and evaluation to observe progress, recognise successes, and identify challenges. This approach facilitates the development of strategies for achieving sustainable results and supports informed decision-making. According to the World Bank (2006), monitoring and evaluation systems are intended to inform project management on whether implementation is proceeding as planned or if corrective action is necessary. A well-designed monitoring and evaluation system provides data on the project's progress and whether it is meeting its objectives. This data may suggest that adjustments are needed to the project to account for changing circumstances in the local environment. Monitoring involves setting key performance indicators (KPIs), gathering data, and analysing it to ensure results are fair and sustainable. Evaluation, on the other hand, involves assessing the impact of programmes and projects to identify areas for improvement. The key differences between monitoring and evaluation are outlined in Table 10.2.

After reviewing the processes for effective monitoring and evaluation, the distinctions between the two are clarified, along with their key indicators.

Table 10.2 The difference between monitoring and evaluation

Subject	Monitoring	Evaluation
Functions	Tracking and project oversight	Assessment
Frequencies	Regularly	Quarterly
Information Sources	Daily observation, reports, weekly or monthly progress reports, review of programmes and projects	The same source of information with monitoring, plus beneficiary and democratic surveys, and special studies
Reports	Project Management	Donors
Methods	Review of reports, administrative databases, registers, and meeting minutes	Research method,
Users	Programmes, projects, and beneficiaries	Outside Stakeholders
Involvement	Staff of the projects and programme, and stakeholders	Experts and external persons
Answers	Milestones completed and results achieved	Why and how the results were achieved

Source Author 2025

The key indicators for monitoring and evaluation are.

1. Continuous: There should be continuous monitoring of programmes and projects throughout the programme or project cycle. This should include regular data collection and project progress tracking that will detect areas for enhancement.
2. Methods: Data should be collected sustainably. The data collected should be analysed by applying appropriate statistical methods. This could involve the use of pictures, maps, GIS information, drones, AI, visual tools, and report writing to communicate complex data and information.
3. Learning and Adjustment: Monitoring and evaluation results and reports should be implemented to inform learning and facilitate adjustments to the project cycle. Such adjustments could be made to activities, targets, and indicators.
4. Progress and Reports: Progress reports, challenges, and results should be communicated to project beneficiaries and stakeholders through various channels such as project and programme meetings, community gatherings, presentations, teams' meetings, reports, and dashboards. This approach helps to confirm that the project outcomes remain relevant and address the needs and priorities of the beneficiaries.
5. Sustainability: Monitoring and evaluation ultimately help ensure the long-term sustainability of programmes and projects. This will be achieved by developing long-term strategies for managing and maintaining project activities and assets that benefit both the project and its beneficiaries.

Monitoring and evaluation play a crucial role in enhancing rural development by refining programmes and projects. They also provide methods to ensure that these initiatives yield tangible and lasting results. By analysing data and information, monitoring progress, providing feedback, encouraging learning and adjustments, and promoting sustainability, monitoring and evaluation enable beneficiaries and stakeholders to make informed decisions about programme and project priorities and resource allocation.

For effective monitoring and evaluation, engaging all stakeholders and communities through a participatory approach is vital. This promotes the sustainable success of projects. Incorporating gender considerations is essential for fairness in addressing gender-related issues. Regularly sharing updates on information, progress, and data with beneficiaries and stakeholders enables the realignment of priorities and the addressing of challenges. Programmes and projects should include quality control measures, with monitoring and evaluation serving as tools for learning and making necessary adjustments to achieve sustainable results. Overall, effective monitoring and evaluation are critical to the success of any programme or project.

1. It effectively helps track rural development progress using programme and project indicators.
2. It helps prioritise sustainable practices and inclusive economic growth, while ensuring fair access to resources.
3. It assists in enhancing service delivery in rural areas by tracking progress, identifying challenges, and ensuring effective governance that fosters sustainable outcomes.
4. It assists in resource allocation, which has a positive impact on the management of programmes and projects.
5. It offers a framework for engaging stakeholders that boosts accountability and transparency.
6. It provides methods to monitor progress, identify areas for improvement, and ensure accountability, thereby guaranteeing quality delivery.
7. It provides data and insights to inform decision-making, leading to effective and sustainable interventions.
8. Monitoring and evaluation help re-strategies to provide better, sustainable programmes and project outcomes.
9. It provides benchmarking for programme and project development, assisting in tracking progress and results.
10. It helps track the budget and flow of funds, enabling sustainable project implementation and management.
11. It is beneficial to demonstrate achieved results by monitoring and evaluating key performance indicators.
12. Effectively monitoring and evaluating rural development programmes and projects is crucial for identifying what works and what does not, and for drawing out valuable lessons. This provides a basis for informed decision-making and improving the effectiveness of rural development performance.
13. It assists in clarifying the objectives of programmes and projects by linking objectives to targets.
14. Enable disadvantaged individuals to participate in and make decisions regarding ongoing rural development programmes and projects.
15. It provides a mechanism to identify challenges, risks, and problems and provides mitigation measures.

16. It allows programme and project managers to identify problems early on and take corrective actions, preventing potential setbacks and ensuring projects stay on track.
17. It establishes a process that identifies challenges and risks and applies corrective action through proper stakeholder engagement and professional input.
18. It provides an avenue to learn through challenges and allows for timely interventions and adjustments to improve outcomes.

The factors listed above are vital for tracking and assessing rural development initiatives. Establishing strategic monitoring and evaluation indicators is crucial for measuring success, sustainability, and the social and economic impact. These indicators are detailed in Table 10.3.

Table 10.3 outlines the key indicators for monitoring and evaluating rural development, aiming to ensure a well-structured and managed rural development that is accountable, transparent, and sustainable. These indicators will help the rural development plan achieve its targets and create a lasting impact on the social and economic progress of rural areas. It is important to highlight that the indicators listed in Table 10.3 are general key indicators used for monitoring and evaluating rural development. Each project or programme should have its own set of specific indicators, which may differ from these but share some similarities. Stakeholders must agree on a set of indicators for each evaluation and monitoring process. The mechanism provides the necessary checks and balances for successful rural development. To achieve the most effective monitoring and evaluation, it will be crucial to recommend policy alignments that support rural development strategies.

10.7 Rural Development Strategic Policy Recommendations

The key policy recommendations for sustainable rural development outlined in this book are presented below.

1. Participatory Approaches: Polices should prioritise affected and interested stakeholders in the policy development process. This means recognising beneficiaries clearly to encourage their participation in planning and decision-making. The policy should support stakeholders by defining participation mechanisms that facilitate the successful delivery of programmes

Table 10.3 Rural development monitoring and evaluation indicators

Strategy	Samples of Indicators
Human Resources and knowledge development	1. Number of schools built 2. Number of people trained, and skills developed 3. Number of schools rehabilitated 4. Number of people who gained access to education 5. Number of people who enrolled on schools 6. Number of people who completed, graduated, or finished with certificates 7. Number of indigenous knowledges transformed and developed
Innovation and Potential development	1. Number of jobs created through innovative ways in the forestry and marine industries 2. Number of Farmers' access to new technologies and innovation 3. Rural businesses and farmers' access to infrastructure such as roads, water, electricity, and how it improves production and income through marketing 4. Number of businesses, SMMEs, Farmers, and production outfits that use drones, GIS, and other IT systems or apps
Production quality and measures	1. Improved crop quality and production 2. Access to regional and international markets 3. Access to government advisory officers
Sustainable use of natural resources	1. Improved Land Usage 2. Amount and number paid out for animal welfare 3. Indicate land developed through afforestation 4. What water and forestry are restored for economic activities 5. Forestry and ecosystem protection that benefits tourism
Diversification of rural economic activities	1. Number of small businesses and SMMEs that have access to finance 2. Access to border marketing and trading 3. Access to storage, packaging, and marketing information 4. Number of youths and women involved in new SMMEs and new businesses 5. New tourism activities and the number of visitors 6. Number of people self-employed through craft 7. Number of new investments in the area

(continued)

Table 10.3 (continued)

Strategy	Samples of Indicators
Rural area standards of living	1. Number of people who have access to basic services 2. Number of Households that have access to basic education and health 3. Are there cultural and traditional activities revitalised that have improved rural economic life? 4. Any training or number of trainings offered to rural households that improve income or economic activities 5. Any community development strategy
Implementing local development strategies	1. Is there sustainable competitiveness and fairness 2. Is there a strategic plan for resource management, and are people involved, and how many people are involved? 3. How many cooperative projects and their impact on household income and effect on the economy 4. Number of skilled people developed and employed in rural areas 5. Policy and strategies developed for rural development by state and local governments 6. Are programmes and projects regarded as transparent and accountable by rural communities? 7. Is there any stakeholder framework developed? 8. Is the sharing of rural development knowledge accessible?
Participation	1. Is there a Stakeholder's Framework Document, and does it include the participation of youths, vulnerable people, and women? 2. Are rural communities and people involved in programme and project identification, initiation, planning, implementation, and monitoring? 3. Is the community participation process a part of the stakeholder framework?
United Nations Sustainable Development Goals	1. Do the rural communities know their role in supporting and implementing the SDGs? 2. Are the rural programmes and projects linked to the SDGs? 3. Are the SDGs key indicators a part of monitoring and evaluation?

(continued)

Table 10.3 (continued)

Strategy	Samples of Indicators
Infrastructure Plans and Development	1. How many rural infrastructure projects were identified, and what was the completion rate? 2. The impact of the rural infrastructure on production, access to market, and human well-being 3. Any Strategic or policy framework for public and private participation in infrastructure development 4. Is there infrastructure that improves cross-border marketing and its impact on production, income, and local economic development? 5. Are there a range of transport options available in rural areas, and do they help lower the cost of travel and production? 6. How many rural populations benefited through the implementation of infrastructure projects, and what types of benefits?
Infrastructure Maintenance	1. Are there facilities and equipment provided by the local authority for maintaining the infrastructure? 2. Are rural communities, organisations, and people involved in infrastructure maintenance, and what are their benefits? 3. Is there any community programme or project for infrastructure maintenance?
Education	1. How many people have access to education and vocational training? 2. How many people have been enrolled in school due to the easy accessibility of education? 3. Is there a new high institution built to increase skills and the workforce? 4. How many people have access to libraries? 5. How many finished with certificates, how many dropped, and why?
Health	1. How many people have access to clinics and hospitals 2. How many people have access to good water and sanitation 3. Are there any mobile clinics or off-site health consultations available, particularly through mobile internet or connections?

(continued)

Table 10.3 (continued)

Strategy	Samples of Indicators
Industry and Special Agro-Industrial Zones	1. How many Special Agro-Industrial Processing Zones (SAPZ) have been created? 2. How many Industries are attracted to SAPZ? 3. Number of jobs created through SAPZ 4. Is there a National Rural Industrial Development Plan? 5. Do they have access to funding at a reasonable rate for industrial development? 6. Do rural industries have access to the global and regional chains? 7. How many industries are in rural areas?
Tourism	1. Is there a Strategic framework for Tourism development and implementation? 2. Are women and youths involved in tourism development and activities? 3. Are there tourism and recreational activities in rural areas? 4. Are there any rural crafts that have been developed to support tourism? 5. Are there tourism guides and locational maps for easy access to tourism activities? 6. Do environmental and cultural conservation initiatives that support tourism have an impact on income and the rural economy?
Smart Rural Communities	1. Are there any innovations or technologies that are enhancing rural life, production, and services? 2. Do rural areas have access to the internet and mobile connections? 3. Does the rural community have access to alternative energy, such as solar farms or wind energy, or government-provided household solar panels? 4. Are there any biocircular green economy initiatives? 5. Do any irrigation and farming facilities run on alternative green energy? 6. Are there water systems powered by alternative green energy? 7. Do internet and mobile phone connections improve rural production and marketing? 8. Does the government provide Wi-Fi to rural Nodes that will cut costs and improve rural production, marketing, services, education, health, good governance, and communication? 9. Do rural areas have access to remote healthcare consultations, online learning, digital libraries, and educational resources? 10. Do rural areas have access to farmers' information online, allowing them to easily check weather conditions and plan farming schedules due to internet and mobile phone accessibility? 11. How many farmers use drones, automated tractors, artificial intelligence, robotics, and blockchains?

and projects. It should also provide opportunities for stakeholders to share their knowledge and expertise.

2. Capacity Building: Polices should offer guidance on investing in capacity-building programmes to enhance skills and talents, and provide resources to oversee rural development initiatives, from planning and implementation to monitoring and evaluation. Skills development should focus on enhancing the competencies of relevant stakeholders, bolstering institutional capacity to address challenges, and keeping pace with emerging technological and innovative trends. Policies should incorporate information and communication technologies as part of capacity building, facilitating connections with regional and global communities. They should also establish mechanisms for all levels of government and government institutions to support capacity-building programmes that benefit their respective rural communities. Additionally, policy should establish systems to enhance the capacity of government civil servants through capacity building, human resource development, and collaboration.
3. Inequality: Policy should include mechanisms to promote gender equality and youth participation in rural development, encompassing the entire process, from initial idea to long-term project planning. It should also ensure equal access to social protection and employment opportunities. Additionally, it should provide a way to protect against discrimination, violence, exploitation, and social and economic abuse.
4. Equitable Access: Policies should clearly define a plan to guarantee equal access to opportunities, participation, and active involvement for young people, women, older adults, and vulnerable individuals. They should support social protection, healthcare, education, vocational training, food security, poverty alleviation, employment, and decent work conditions. Moreover, policies should foster human capital development through increased educational access and promote well-being by ensuring access to quality healthcare services. They should also include mechanisms to guarantee fair resource distribution and safeguard measures for marginalised groups.
5. Financial Assistance: Polices should promote financial mechanisms for social guardians, including health coverage and early childhood care for vulnerable families. This should be accompanied by mechanisms for disaster risk reduction, climate change adaptation, and social pensions through strategic partnerships.

6. Environmental Sustainability: Policies should align with international and regional standards to advance environmental sustainability. They should promote the sustainable utilisation of natural resources, safeguard cultural heritage, and protect sensitive environmental zones. This encompasses support for water resource management, afforestation, and biodiversity conservation. A mechanism is essential to foster positive economic, social, and environmental links between urban and rural areas. Furthermore, a system should be established to strengthen rural capacity for planning, executing, and managing climate change adaptation and mitigation, as well as environmental protection and management.
7. Policy mechanisms need to be established to support the development of standards that are integrated through evaluation tools, data management, and information systems. The policy should also emphasise resilience principles across risk reduction, awareness, response, recovery, and remediation efforts. Additionally, the standards should encourage linkages and synergy among initiatives related to disaster risk reduction, climate change adaptation and mitigation, humanitarian programmes, and sustainable development.
8. Emergency Response System: Policies should enhance the capacities of rural communities, local governments, and the rural population to respond to all health-related hazards and emerging threats by providing funds, policy direction, and strategies.
9. Social Sustainability: Policy should aim to promote social cohesion and community development by encouraging inclusive and peaceful relationships within rural communities. It should support cultural activities that foster community bonding and attract visitors to the area. Additionally, it should outline the needs of vulnerable groups, such as the elderly, women, and young people in rural areas, including those with disabilities. The policy should also provide a precise mechanism for how these groups can benefit from rural programmes and projects.
10. Financial System: Implement insurance and finance systems to support disaster management, enhance access to essential resources such as food, water, and energy, and strengthen social security networks during crises, thereby making resources more accessible, affordable, and sustainable.
11. Promote a Culture of Entrepreneurship: Many policies tend to overlook the role of mentoring in rural areas, particularly in the context of business and entrepreneurship. Consequently, rural development strategies should incorporate a system for responsible mentoring in these regions. Additionally, policies should promote startup funding for rural entrepreneurs, taking into account the specific needs of young people and women.

These policy recommendations are crucial for achieving sustainable rural development and aligning with a strategic objective. They help to ensure that rural development is comprehensive, aligns with the strategy's aims, and remains sustainable over the long term. Ultimately, the goal is to promote and harness rural development for social and economic progress, environmental sustainability, and good governance.

Conclusion

11

Rural development extends beyond merely boosting agricultural output; it emphasises comprehensive social and economic progress to ensure sustainable livelihoods for rural populations. Rural development embodies a lifestyle closely linked to the local environment, culture, traditional practices, daily routines, social interactions, and economic activities. The strategic framework provided offers pathways for African countries to pursue sustainable growth. Recognising the diverse social and economic assets of rural areas and their connections to urban, regional, and global markets is crucial for sustainable development. As Van der Ploeg et al. (2000) noted, rural development is primarily an autonomous process influenced by local stakeholders. Consequently, supporting a bottom-up approach is crucial for sustaining rural development initiatives, plans, and implementations. Various actors, including NGOs, the private sector, international organisations, and local communities, should be involved in developing policies and strategies, and this responsibility is not solely on the government. Southeastern Nigeria exemplifies how individuals and communities can lead rural development efforts to achieve socio-economic advancement.

To promote sustainable rural development, challenges such as demographic shifts to cities, limited skills development, and unemployment, which threaten rural progress, must be addressed. Other challenges that threaten rural development as listed are weak leadership due to poor policy-making, limited access to funding and credit, low household incomes that hinder meeting basic needs, infrastructure issues such as unreliable electricity and water supplies, poorly maintained roads, inadequate health facilities, limited access to quality healthcare and insurance, underfunded schools, literacy issues, land use and tenure conflicts, transportation shortages, and environmental challenges. Case studies demonstrate

C. Osuigwe, *Economic Development of Rural Areas*, Sustainable Development Goals Series, https://doi.org/10.1007/978-3-032-10572-1_11

that providing basic infrastructure, such as education, healthcare, roads, water, sanitation, and electricity, will empower rural communities, create jobs, support local businesses and small industries, and promote sustainable rural development.

Reorganising service delivery through a clear, actionable plan is vital for effective rural planning, which boosts the rural economy and supports overall national development. Using monitoring and evaluation tools will help ensure the sustainability of rural development and aid in reaching short-term, medium-term, and long-term objectives, especially after project completion. Unlocking Africa's rural potential successfully depends on comprehensive rural development strategies that guarantee access to key resources, infrastructure, and social and economic amenities—all essential for sustainable, long-term growth across the continent.

Land ownership remains a barrier to rural progress. Limited access to land creates significant inequalities, trapping many in poverty. Rural communities should have access to private land ownership and title deeds to boost income and promote rural development. This approach will promote social benefits such as environmental conservation and sustainable tourism. By applying the suggested strategies, rural-urban disparities can be narrowed, and poverty alleviated by empowering rural communities to engage actively and develop innovative methods to diversify social and economic activities. Furthermore, it will aid in conserving natural resources and ecosystems that are essential for sustainable social and economic growth.

The book emphasises that reorganising service delivery through a clear and actionable plan is essential for effective rural planning, which boosts the rural economy and supports overall national growth. Additionally, rural development efforts must be continuously monitored and evaluated to ensure sustainability and meet short-term, medium-term, and long-term objectives, especially after project completion. This approach will unlock Africa's rural potential by providing access to vital resources, infrastructure, and social and economic amenities, all of which are critical for sustained growth across the continent. Various theories and literature advocate different strategies for planning and implementing rural development. The focus should shift towards a holistic and integrated approach that promotes better cooperation among government levels and reduces bureaucratic barriers, making comprehensive rural development achievable, fostering economic diversification and the emergence of smart rural communities.

References

Abass, I. M. (1993). The Challenge of Rural Development Strategies in a Deregulated Economy. Paper prepared for a National Seminar on Rural Development-Doing More Less Developing Rural Resources in a Deregulated Economy-Organized by New Nigerian Newspapers Limited in collaboration with Arthur Green Consultants Held at Shiroro Hotel Minna, Niger State from 10th–12th February.

Abdu, M. S., & Marshall, R. (1990). Agriculture and Development Policy: A Critical Review of Nigerian Experience in the Period Up to 1985. *Journal of Rural Studies, 6*(3), 311–323.

Adesina, A., (2018). Unlocking Africa's Agricultural Potential to Create Wealth. President, Africa Development Bank at the Public Lecture of the Food and Agriculture Organization (FAO) of the United Nations, Held at the FAO Head Office, Rome, Italy, August 27, 2018.

AFDB—African Development Bank. (2023). *Africa's Infrastructure: Great Potential But Little Impact on Positive Growth*. https://www.afdb.org/fileadmin/uploads/afdb/Documents/Publications/2018AEO/African_Economic_Outlook_2018_-_EN_Chapter3.pdf

Ajaegbu, H. I. (1977). *Urban and Rural Development in Nigeria*. Hienman Press.

Alkire, S., Kanagaratnam, U., & Suppa, N. (2021). The global Multidimensional Poverty Index (MPI) 2021. OPHI MPI Methodological Note 51, Oxford Poverty and Human Development Initiative, University of Oxford.

Alston, P. (2005). Ships Passing in the Night: The Current State of Human Rights and Development Debate Seen Through the Lens of the Millennium Development Goals. *Human Rights Quarterly*., *27*(3), 755–829

Angelsen, A., Jagger, P., Babigumira, R., Belcher, B., Hogarth, N. J., Bauch, S., Rner, J. B., & Wunder, S. (2014). Environmental Income and Rural Livelihoods: A Global-Comparative Analysis. *World Development, 64*, S12–S28. https://doi.org/10.1016/j.worlddev.2014.03.006

Arkhangelskaia, A., & Perfilyeva, E. (2023). *Workshop on the Design of the National Human Development Report on Energy Vulnerabilities in the Kyrgyz Republic*. United Nations. https://www.undp.org/sites/g/files/zskgke326/files/2023-02/CK_Slides_FINAL_ENG.pdf

AU. (2015). *Agenda 2063: The Africa We Want. Framework Document*. Retrieved January 19, 2025, from https://au.int/sites/default/files/documents/33126-doc-framework_document_book.pdf

C. Osuigwe, *Economic Development of Rural Areas*, Sustainable Development Goals Series, https://doi.org/10.1007/978-3-032-10572-1

Azolibe, C. B., & Okonkwo, J. J. (2020). Infrastructure Development and Industrial Sector Productivity in Sub-Saharan Africa. *Journal of Economics and Development*. https://doi.org/10.1108/JED-11-2019-0062

Badiora, A. I. (2020). *Perceptions on Corruption and Compliance in the Administration of Town Planning Laws: The Experience from Lagos Metropolitan Area, Nigeria*. Retrieved January 18, 2025, from https://journals.ufs.ac.za/index.php/trp/article/view/4505

Bakre, O. R. (2022). *Rural Developmental Initiatives in the Post-apartheid South Africa: A Case Study on Poverty Alleviation in Mgobodzi, Lusikisiki Mcobothini and Gunjaneni* (Doctoral dissertation)

Basler, A., & Brunswick, V. (1979). The Concept of Integrated Rural Development, Intereconomics, ISSN 0020-5346, Verlag Weltarchiv, Hamburg, Vol. 14, No. 4, pp. 190–195, https://doi.org/10.1007/BF02924277

Borys T. (2016). Aksjologiczne podstawy zrównoważonego i inteligentnego rozwoju (Axiological Foundations of Sustainable and Smart Growth). *Ekonomia Środowiska/Economics of the Environment, 3*(58), 33–46.

Byamugisha, F. F. K. (2013). (forthcoming). *Securing Africa's Land for Shared Prosperity: A Program to Scale Up Reforms and Investments*. World Bank, Sustainable Development Department, Africa Regional Vice-presidency.

CAC. (2024). *Corporate Affairs Commission Public Notice List of Struck Off Companies*. https://www.cac.gov.ng/wp-content/uploads/2024/01/STRUCK_OFF_FINAL_LIST_2024.pdf

Castro-Arce, K., & Vanclay, F. (2020). Transformative Social Innovation for Sustainable Rural Development: An Analytical Framework to Assist Community-Based Initiatives. *Journal of Rural Studies, 74*, 45–54.

Camara-Leret, R., & Dennhy, Z. (2019). Indigenous Knowledge of New Guinea's Useful Plants. A Review. *Economic Botany, 73*(3): 405–415. https://doi.org/10.1007/s12231-019-09464-1

Chakamera, C. (2021). Qualitative and Quantitative Effects of Infrastructure on Economic Growth and Productivity in Africa. *Journal of Construction and Built Environment, 1*(1), 26–50.

Chenery, H., Ahluwalia, M. S., Bell, C. L. G., Duloy, J. H., & Jolly, R. (1974). Income Inequality: Some Dimensions of the Problem. In *Redistribution with Growth by*. Oxford University Press.

Cloke, P., & Park, C. C. (1985). *Rural Resource Management*. Croom Helm.

Coman, A., & Ronen, B. (2009). Focused SWOT: Diagnosing Critical Strengths and Weaknesses. *International Journal of Production Research, 47*(20), 5677–5689.

Cowie, P., Townsend, L., & Salemink, K. (2020). Smart Rural Futures: Will Rural Areas Be Left Behind in the 4th Industrial Revolution? *Journal of Rural Studies, 79*,169–176. https://doi.org/10.1016/j.jrurstud.2020.08.042.

Damiani, O. (1999). *Beyond Market Failures: Irrigation, the State, and Non-Traditional Agriculture in Northeast Brazil* (PhD dissertation). Massachusetts Institute of Technology.

Damiani, O. (2008). *Rural Development from a Territorial Perspective Case Studies in Asia and Latin America*. Retrieved January 31, 2025, from https://openknowledge.worldbank.org/server/api/core/bitstreams/424909af-60f2-53ed-b573-433b4d2d8c8f/content

Dethier, J. J. (2015). Infrastructure in Africa. In C. Monga & J. Y. Lin (Eds.), *The Oxford Handbook of Africa and Economics, Vol. 2: Policies and Practices*. Oxford University Press.

DFFE (….). *Climate Change Adaptation Human Settlements, Adaptation Scenarios Factsheet Series, Factsheet 4 of 7*. https://www.dffe.gov.za/sites/default/files/reports/research/ccaq/ltas_ph2factsheet4climateadaptation_humansettlements.pdf

Dollar, D., & Kraay, A. (2002). Growth Is Good for the Poor. *Journal of Economic Growth, 7*(3), 195–225.

Douwe, J., Renting, H., Brunori, G., Knickei, K., Mannion, J., Marsden, T., de Roest, K., Sevilla-Guzmán, E., & Ventura, F. (2017). Rural Development: From Practices and Policies Towards Theory. In T. Marsden, J. Banks, & G. Bristow (Eds.), *The Routledge Handbook of Rural Studies* (pp. 201–218). Routledge. https://doi.org/10.4324/9781315237213-11

DRDLR. (2009). The Comprehensive Rural Development Programme Framework. Department: Rural Development and Land Reform Republic of South Africa. 20 Steve Biko former (Beatrix) Street, Agriculture Place, Arcadia, Pretoria.

DRDLR. (2014). National Rural Youth Service Corps (NARYSEC). Department: Rural Development and Land Reform Republic of South Africa. 20 Steve Biko former (Beatrix) Street, Agriculture Place, Arcadia, Pretoria.

DRDLR. (2019). DRDLR Organisational Structure Presentation to The Portfolio Committee on Rural Development and Land Reform. Department: Rural Development and Land Reform Republic of South Africa. 20 Steve Biko former (Beatrix) Street, Agriculture Place, Arcadia, Pretoria.

DRDLR. (2023). The Integrated Rural Development Sector Strategy. Department: Rural Development and Land Reform Republic of South Africa. 20 Steve Biko former (Beatrix) Street, Agriculture Place, Arcadia, Pretoria.

Egonmwan, J. A., & Ibodje, S. W. E. (2001). *Developmental Administration Theory and Practice Benin City*. Resyin (Nig) Company Ltd.

ElGanainy, A. A., Hakobyan, S., Liu, F., Weisfeld, H., Allard, C., Balima, H. W., Bteish, C., Giri, R., Kanda, D. S., Meleshchuk, S., Ramirez, G., Zymek, R., Arora, V. B., Lall, S., Kett, B. R., & Pohl, M. M. (2023). *Trade Integration in Africa: Unleashing the Continent's Potential in a Changing World* (Departmental Paper No. 2023/003). International Monetary Fund. https://doi.org/10.5089/9798400232794.087.A001

EPRS. (2017).*Global Trends to 2035: Geo-Politics and International Power*. European Parliamentary Research Service.https://doi.org/10.2861/800293

Fatile, J. O., Fajonyomi, S. O., & Adejuwon, K. D. (2017). State-Local Government Fiscal Relations and Grassroots Development: An Empirical Review of Selected Local Governments in Lagos State. *Journal of Public Administration, Finance and Law, 12*(1), 72–85.

FAO. (2009). *State of the World's Forests 2009*. Retrieved February 10, 2025, from https://www.fao.org/4/i0350e/i0350e00.htm

FAO & UNEP. (2020). *The State of the World's Forests 2020. Forests, Biodiversity and People* (214 p.). FAO and UNEP. https://doi.org/10.4060/ca8642en

Florin, M., & Latu, C. (2020). Sustainable Rural Development Under Agenda 2030. In M. J. Bastante-Ceca (Ed.), *Sustainability Assessment at the 21st Century* (pp. 9–18). InTech.

Filani, M. O. (1993). Transport and Rural Development in Nigeria. *Journal of Transport Geography, 1*(4), 248–254.

FS (….). Rural Development. Programme 8. Retrieved February 10, 2025, from https://www.ard.fs.gov.za/?page_id=539

Galal, S. (2024). *Share of Rural Population in Africa 2000–2023*. Retrieved January 25, 2025, from https://www.statista.com/statistics/1491165/africa-share-of-rural-population/

Gondo, P. C. (2010). *Financing of Sustainable Forest Management in Africa: An Overview of the Current Situation and Experiences*. Southern Alliance for Indigenous Resources (SAFIRE). Retrieved February 2, 2025, from https://www.un.org/esa/forests/wp-content/uploads/2014/12/Africa_case_study.pdf

Gretton, P., & Salma, U. (1996). *Land Degradation and the Australian Agricultural Industry* (Industry Commission Staff Information Paper, AGPs, Canberra).

Guzal-Dec, D., & Zwolińska-Ligaj, M. (2017). The Role of Local Action Groups in the Process of Multifunctional Development of a Peripheral Region. *A Case Study of the Region of Lublin, Poland, Wieś i Rolnictwo, 3*(176), 97–120.

Habib, I. (2018). *Education for Rural People in Africa: Policy, Practice, and Lessons Learned*. UNESCO. Retrieved June 14, 2025, from https://unesdoc.unesco.org/ark:/48223/pf0000366512

Haller, A. P. (2012). Concept of Economic Growth And Development. Challenges of Crises and of Knowledge. *Economy Transdisciplinarity Cognition, 15*(1), 66–71.

Harris, R. R. (….). *The Healthcare Crisis in Sub-Saharan Africa*. Retrieved June 14, 2025, from https://africanmissionhealthcare.org/the-healthcare-crisis-in-sub-saharan-africa/

Hausermann, H., Ferring, D.,Atosona, B., Mentz,G.,Amankwah, R.,Chang, A.,Hartfield, K.,Effah, E.,Asuamah, G. Y.,Mansell, C., & Sastri, N. (2018, August). Land-Grabbing, Land-Use Transformation and Social Differentiation: Deconstructing "Small-Scale" in Ghana's Recent Gold Rush. World Development, *108*, 103–114. https://doi.org/10.1016/j.worlddev.2018.03.014

Helms, M. M., & Nixon, J. (2010). Exploring SWOT Analysis—Where Are We Now? A Review Of Academic Research from the Last Decade. *Journal of Strategy & Management, 3*(3), 215–251.

Holden, S. T., Deininger, K., & Ghebru, H. (2011). Tenure Security, Gender, Low-Cost Land Certification and Land Rental Market Participation in Ethiopia. *Journal of Development Studies, 47*(1), 31–47.

Hosseini,S., Frank,L., Fridgen,G., & Heger,S. (2018). Do Not Forget About Smart Towns: How to Bring Customized Digital Innovation to Rural Areas. *Business and Information Systems Engineering, 60*,243–257. https://doi.org/10.1007/s12599-018-0536-2

Houngbo, G. (2014). The Need to Invest in Africa's Rural Transformation. International Labour Organization, 4 route des Morillons, CH-1211 Geneva 22, Switzerland.

Ibetan, J., & Oghator, E. (2013). Trends of Development Planning in Nigeria. *A Journal of Sustainable Development in Africa*, 15(4). ISSN 1520-5509 Clarion University of Pennsylvania. Clarioe, Pennsylvania.

IFAD. (2011). *Rural Poverty in Nigeria*. International Fund for Agricultural Development. http://www.ruralpovertyportal.org/web/guest/country/home/tags/nigeria

ILO (2020). *Global Wage Report 2020–21: Wages and Minimum Wages in the Time of COVID-19 Flagship Rep*. International Labour Organization, Geneva.

ILO. (2023). *Social Justice for Rural Populations Means Prosperity for the Planet*. Retrieved February 17, 2025, from https://webapps.ilo.org/infostories/en-GB/Stories/Employment/rural-economies#introduction

Irwin, E. G., Isserman, A. M., Kilkenny, M., & Partridge, M. D. (2010). A Century of Research on Rural Development and Regional Issues. *American Journal of Agricultural Economics, 92*(2), 522–553.

Iwuagwu, O. (2006). Rural Development in Eastern Nigeria: An Assessment of Colonial and Post-colonial Development Plans in the Former Owerri Province, 1946–1976. *Lagos Historical Review, 6*, 118–132.

Jerome, A. (2011). Infrastructure, Economic Growth and Poverty Reduction in Africa. *Journal of Infrastructure Development, 3*(2), 127–151. https://doi.org/10.1177/097493061100300203

Janssen-Jansen, L. B. (2008). Space for Space, a Transferable Development Rights Initiative for Changing the Dutch Landscape. *Landscape and Urban Planning, 87*(3), 192–200. https://doi.org/10.1016/j.landurbplan.2008.06.002

John, A. (2020). *The Forgotten Farmer-Herdsmen Conflict in Nigeria's 'Middle Belt'*. Retrieved June 11, 2025, from https://www.msf.org.za/news-and-resources/latest-news/forgotten-farmer-herdsmen-conflict-nigeria-s-middle-belt

Johnson, J. M. F.,Franzluebbers, A. J.,Weyers, S. L.,Donald, C., & Reicosky, D. C. (2007). *Agricultural Opportunities to Mitigate Greenhouse Gas Emissions*. Retrieved February 8, 2025, from https://www.sciencedirect.com/science/article/abs/pii/S0269749107003016

Jutting, J., Corsi, E., Kauffmann, C., Mcdonnell, I., Osterrieder, H., Pinaud, N., & Wegner, L. (2005). What Makes Decentralisation in Developing Countries Pro-Poor? *The European Journal of Development Research, 17*(4), 626–648.

Kakupa, P., Tembo, P., & Daka, H. (2015). Linking Teacher Effectiveness to School Performance: Evidence from Rural Day Secondary Schools in the Western Province of Zambia.*International Journal of Educational Development, 40*, 100–112.

Kaiser, N., & Barstow, C. K. (2022). Rural Transportation Infrastructure in Low- and Middle-Income Countries: A Review of Impacts, Implications, and Interventions. *Sustainability, 14*, 2149. https://doi.org/10.3390/su14042149.

Kakumba, U., & Nsingo, S. (2008). Citizen Participation in Local Government and the Process of Rural Development: The Rhetoric and Reality of Uganda. *Journal of Public Administration, 43*(2), 107–123.

Kane, M., & Sand, P. (1988). *Economic Development: What Works at the Local Level*. National League of Cities.

Kerr, K.(1990).*Crafts Development Potential in the Outer Islands and Forestry Regions of Indonesia*.Report on a Consultancy for the Forestry Studies Project, UTF/INS/65 (Unpublished).

Khan, M. H. (2001). *Rural Poverty in Developing Countries Implications for Public Policy*. International Monetary Fund. The Economic Issues, No 26.

Khumalo, M. J., Choga, I., & Elias, M. E. (2017). Challenges Associated with Infrastructure Delivery. *Public and Municipal Finance (Hybrid), 6*(2), 35–45. https://doi.org/10.21511/pmf.06(2).2017.04

Koreman, M. C. J., & Altes, W. K. K. (2023). Re-using Vacant Farm Buildings for Commercial Purposes: Two Cases from the Netherlands. Delft University of Technology (TU Delft), Faculty of Architecture and the Built Environment, Department of Management and the Built Environment, Land Development, Julianalaan 134, 2628 BL Delft, Netherlands.

Kosiedowski, W. (2016). *Koncepcja rozwoju inkluzywnego i jej realizacja w Europie Środkowo-Wschodniej*. Rocznik Instytutu Europy Środkowo-Wschodniej, 5, 74. Retrieved from http://www.iesw.lublin.pl/rocznik/articles/RIESW_17321395_14-5-276.pdf (in Polish).

Kufakwandi, F. S. (2000). *Consortium Funding for Sustainable Forest Management: African Perspectives and Priorities*. African Development Bank.

Krikẹlas, A. C. (1992). *Why Regions Grow: A Review of Research on the Economic-Base Model* (pp. 16–29). Economic Review Federal Reserve Bank of Atlanta.

Kyriacou, A. P., Muinelo-Gallo, L., & Roca-Sagalés, O. (2015). Fiscal Decentralization and Regional Disparities. *Regional Science, 94*(1), 89–107. https://doi.org/10.1111/pirs.12061

Lankford, S. V., Grybovych, O., & Lankford, J. K. (2008). Context for Peace and Community Tourism: A Worldview Framework. *World Leisure Journal, 50*(3), 199–208. https://doi.org/10.1080/04419057.2008.9674553

Leigland, J., & Roberts, A. (2007). *The African Project Preparation Gap: Africans Address a Critical Limiting Factor in Infrastructure Investment* (World Bank Publications—Reports 10716). The World Bank Group.

Lui, A. (2024). *Fuelling Africa's Infrastructure Growth: Alternative Funding*. Cyda & Co.

Making Finance Work for Africa. *Policy Brief: On Agricultural Finance in Africa*. Retrieved May, from http://www.mfw4a.org/agriculturalrural-finance/agricultural-rural-finance.html.

McKinsey Global Institute. (2010). *Lions on the Move: The Progress and Potential of African Economies*. http://www.mckinsey.com/Insights/MGI/Research/Productivity_Competitiveness_and_Growth/Lions_on_the_move

Malchow, N., & Waldmann, A. (2017, March). The Development Potential of Cross-Border Infrastructure in Africa: A Job Creation Perspective. *Bridges Africa, 6*(2). International Centre for Trade and Sustainable Development. Geneva, Switzerland.

Marcellus, I. O. (2009). Development Planning in Nigeria: Reflections on the National Economic Empowerment and Development Strategy (NEEDS), 2003-2007. *Journal of Social Sciences, 20*(3), 197–210.

Marsden, P. C., & Mooney, T. (2006). *Handbook of Rural Studies*. SAGE. ISBN 978-1-4462-0694-2.

Martinez-Vazquez, J., Lago-Peñas, S., & Sacchi, A. (2016). The Impact of Fiscal Decentralization: A Survey. *Journal of Economic Surveys, 31*(4), 1095–1129. https://doi.org/10.1111/joes.12182

Mijindadi, N. B. (1978, January). Integrated Rural Development: Concept and Planning Implications—With Examples from Nigeria. *Community Development Journal, 13*(1), 21–28.

Miller, D. C., Ordoñez, P. J., Brown, S. E., Forrest, S., Nava, N. J., Hughes, K., & Baylis, K. (2020). The Impacts of Agroforestry on Agricultural Productivity, Ecosystem Services, and Human Well-Being in Low- and Middle-Income Countries: An Evidence and Gap Map. *Campbell Systematic Reviews, 16*(1), 1066. https://doi.org/10.1002/cl2.1066

Monticelli, F., Day, C., Barron, P., Haynes, R., & Smith, J., & Sello, E. (2010). *District Health Barometer 2008/09*. Health Systems Trust.

Morris, M., Binswanger-Mkhize, H. P., & Derek, B. D. (2009). *Awakening Africa's Sleeping Giant: Prospects for Commercial Agriculture in the Guinea Savannah Zone and Beyond*. World Bank.

Moseley, J. (2003). *Rural Development: Principles and Practice*. SAGE.

Myrdal, G. M. (1957). *Economic Theory and Urban Development Region*. Gerald Duckworth.

NDIC. https://ndic.gov.ng/failure-resolution/closed-financial-institutions/

NDIC. (….). *Closed Financial Institutions*. https://ndic.gov.ng/failure-resolution/closed-financial-institutions/

Nekwaya, J. H. (2007). *Assessing Community Participation in Development Planning and Service Delivery. A Case Study of the Omusati Regional Council* (Master's Thesis). University of Stellenbosch.

Nel, E. L. (2019). *Regional and Local Economic Development in South Africa: The Experience of the Eastern Cape*. Routledge.

NEPAD. (….). *Transforming Africa. NEPAD in Brief*. Retrieved January 21, 2025, from https://www.nepad.org/publication/nepad-brief#:~:text=The%20New%20Partnership%20for%20Africa's,ICT%2C%20Capacity%20Development%20and%20Communications

Nicolaides, A., & Dludla, N. (2023). *Sustainable Rural Development and Socio-Economic Upliftment of Marginalised Communities in South Africa by*. https://papers.ssrn.com/sol3/papers.cfm?abstract_id=4396265

Nhlakanipho, S. (2010). *An Investigation of Community Participation Trends in the Rural Development Process in Nquthu, Northern KwaZulu-Natal* (M.CW. Dissertation). University of Zululand. https://hdl.handle.net/10530/600

Nyerere, J. (1977). *The Arusha Declaration: Ten Years After*. Government Printer.

Nwokwu, P. M., Ndukwe, C., & Ode, S. I. (2023). Effect of State and Local Government Fiscal Relations on Rural Development in Ebonyi State Nigeria (2015–2021). *Journal of Policy and Development Studies (JPDS), 13*(4), 2814–1091. ISSN(p) 0189-5958 ISSN (e).

Nwokoro, C. V., & Chima, F. O. (2017). Impact of Environment Degradation on Agricultural Production and Poverty in Rural Nigeria. *American International Journal of Contemporary Research, 7*(2), 6–14.

Okoli, F. C. (2004). *Theory and Practice of Public of Public Organizations. A Book of Readings*. John Jacobs Classical Publishers Limited.

Olar, A., & Jitea, M. I. (2021). Constrains of the Multi-Sectoral Partnerships in Romania-Are Local Action Groups Sustainable? *Advanced Research in Life Sciences, 5*(1), 43–47.

Onah, F. O. (2006). *Managing Public Programmes and Projects*. Nsukka Great A, P, Express Publishers Ltd.

Organisation for Economic Co-operation and Development (OECD). (2003). *The Future of Rural Policy: From Sectoral to Place-Based Policies in Rural Areas*. OECD Publications.

Osabohien, R., Oluwatoyin, M., Obindah, G., Ogunbiyi, T., & Ebere Nwosu, E. (2019, June). Agriculture Development, Employment Generation and Poverty Reduction in West Africa. *The Open Agriculture Journal*. Research Article. https://doi.org/10.2174/1874331501913010082

Osuigwe, C. E. (1996). *Identification of Growth Potentials for Rural Development: A Case Study of Ahiazu Mbaise Local Government Area*. Abia State University.

Osuigwe, C. E. (2011). *Shopping Leakage: Case Study of Maseru: Shopping/Consumer Behaviour, Retail Space, Thinking Planning in a Retail Environment and Government and Institutional Impact in a Retail Institution.* VDM Verleg, Dr. Muller.

Osuigwe, C. E. (2024). *Leadership and Economic Development Challenges in Post-Colonial Africa. Creating Inclusive Economic Growth.* Palgrave Macmillan, Gewerbestrasse, 11, 63330, Cham, Switzerland.

Park,C., & Cha,J.A. (2019). Trend on Smart Village and Implementation of Smart Village Platform. *International Journal of Advanced Smart Convergence, 8*, 177–183. https://doi.org/10.7236/IJASC.2019.8.3.177

Petukhova, M. S., Rudoy, E. V., Nadezhda, V., & Orlova, N. V. (2023). Key Trends of Rural Development in the World and Their Projection in Russia. *Russian Journal of Economics, 9*(4), 336–350.

Papaioannou, T. (2014). How Inclusive Can Innovation and Development Be in the Twenty-First Century? *Innovation and Development, 4*(2), 187–202.

Philippe, P., & Jean-François Ruault, J. F. (2010). *Economic-Base Theory and Highly Open Economies: Incorporating Day-to-Day Mobility.* Retrieved March 18, 2025, from hal-02269336. HAL Id: hal-02269336. https://hal.science/hal-02269336v1

Phiri, M. Z., Molotja, N., Makelane, H., Kupamupindi, T., & Ndinda, C. (2016). Inclusive Innovation and Inequality in South Africa: A Case for Transformative Social Policy. *Innovation and Development, 6*(1), 123–139.

Plaizier, W. (2016). *How Africa Can Feed the World.* Retrieved 5 May 2020, from https://www.weforum.org/agenda/2016/01/how-africa-can-feed-the-world

Pahle, S. (2015). Stepchildren of Liberation: South African Farm Workers' Elusive Rights to Organise and Bargain Collectively. *Journal of Southern African Studies, 41*, 1121–1140.

Pye, E. A. (1988). *Artisans in Economic Development.* International Development Research Centre.

Place, F., & Otsuka, K. (2002). Land Tenure Systems and Their Impacts on Agricultural Investments and Productivity in Uganda. *Journal of Development Studies, 38*(6), 105–128.

Reed, M. S. (2008). Stakeholder Participation for Environmental Management: A Literature Review. *Biological Conservation, 141*, 2417–2431.

Schrrre, G. (1996). Population Pressure and Land Degradation: The Case of Ethiopia. *145 Journal of Environmental Economics and Management, 30*(0002).

Sebunya, K. (2024). *Conservation and Tourism: Africa's Keys to Unlocking a Sustainable Future.* African Wildlife Foundation.

Sekabira, H., & Qaim, M. (2017). Mobile Money, Agricultural Marketing, and Off-Farm Income in Uganda. *Agricultural Economics,48*, 597–611. Retrieved February 2, 2025, fromhttps://doi.org/10.1111/AGEC.12360

Seuyong, F. T., Silwal, A. R., Begazo, T., Newhouse, D., & N'Ghauran, A. (2023). *The Size and Distribution of Digital Connectivity Gaps in Sub-Saharan Africa.* International Bank for Reconstruction and Development/The World Bank. 1818 H Street NW Washington DC 20433.

Signe, L. (2018). *18 Africa's Consumer Market Potential: Trends, Drivers, Opportunities, and Strategies.* Retrieved February 10, 2025, from https://www.brookings.edu/wp-content/uploads/2018/12/Africas-consumer-market-potential.pdf

Sizani, S. P. (2012). *Comprehensive Rural Development Programme: Departmental Briefing, Committee Report and Minutes Adoption.* Land Reform and Rural Development. https://pmg.org.za/committee-meeting/14352/

Sustainable Development in Communities Indicators for Smart Cities (Under Development), Standard ISO ISO/CD 37122, International Organization for Standardization, 2018, February 2018. [Online]. Available: https://www.iso.org/standard/69050.html

Swaans, K., Boogaard, B., Bendapudi, R., Taye, H., Hendrickx, S., & Klerkx, L. (2014). Operationalizing Inclusive Innovation: Lessons from Innovation Platforms in Livestock Value Chains in India and Mozambique. *Innovation and Development, 4*(2), 239–257.

Tambo, J. A., Aliamo, C., Davis, T., Mugambi, I., Romney, D., Onyango, D. O., Kansimme, M., Alokit, S. T., & Byantwale, S. T. (2019). The Impact of ICT-Enabled Extension Campaign on Farmers' Knowledge and Management of Fall Armyworm in Uganda. *International Journal of Agricultural Sustainability, 19*(5–6), 566–582.

Tao, R., & Xu, Z. (2007). Urbanization, Rural Land System and Social Security for Migrants in China.*The Journal of Development Studies, 43*, 1301–1320.

Tiebout, C.-M. (1956). Exports and Regional Economic Growth. *The Journal of Political Economy, 64*(2), 160–164.

Thusi, X., & Mlambo, V. H. (2023). The Effects of Africa's Infrastructure Crisis and Its Root Causes. *International Journal of Environmental, Sustainability, and Social Science, 4*(4), 1055–1067.

Todaro, M. P., & Smith, S. C. (2015). *Economic Development* (12th ed.). Pearson Education Limited.

Tong, W., & Lo, K. (2021). *Back to the Countryside: Rural Development and the Spatial Patterns of Population Migration in Zhejiang, China.* Retrieved January 30, 2025, from https://www.mdpi.com/2077-0472/11/8/788

Traoré, M., Hilson, G., & Hilson, A. (2024). Reimagining Entrepreneurship in the Artisanal and Small-Scale Mining Sector: Fresh Insights from Sub-Saharan Africa. *Africa Journal of Management, 10*(2), 176–207. https://doi.org/10.1080/23322373.2024.2349481

Raghumani, N. (2012). Christian Missionaries and Their Impact on Socio—Cultural Development—Undivided Koraput District a Study. *Journal of Humanities and Social Science, 2*(3), 01–05.

Rogers, E. M., & Svenning, L. (Eds.) (1969). *Modernization Among Peasants: Impact of Communication.* Holt, Rinechart and Winston.

Rosenstein-Rodan, P. N. (1943). Problems of Industrialisation of Eastern and South-Eastern Europe. *The Economic Journal, 53*(210–211), 202–211.

Ugwu, C. E. (2009). The Imperatives of National Development Programmes Harmonization in Nigeria: Vision 2020, Millennium Development Goals and seven Point Agenda. *Nigerian Journal of Public Administration and Local Government (UNN), XIV*(2), 200–216.

United Nations. (2015). *Goal 2: Zero Hunger.* United Nations Sustainable Development 2023. Retrieved October 15, 2025, fromhttps://www.un.org/sustainabledevelopment/hunger/

United Nations. (2017). *Unpacking Sustainable Development Goal 4 Education 2030.* United Nations Educational, Scientific and Cultural Organization. ED-16/ESC-PCR/GD/1(REV. Oct. 2017). Retrieved January 20, 2025, from https://docs.campaignforeducation.org/post2015/SDG4.pdf

United Nations. (2018). *Sustainable Development Goal 6 Synthesis Report on Water and Sanitation.* Published by the United Nations New York, New York 10017, United States of America.

United Nations. (2021). *Reducing Poverty and Inequality in Rural Areas: Key to Inclusive Development.* Retrieved March 19, 2025, from https://social.desa.un.org/sites/default/files/migrated/22/2021/08/PB_106-1.pdf

United Nations Development Programme. (2015). *Human Development Report 2015: Work for Human Development.* Retrieved March 1, 2025, from http://report.hdr.undp.org/

United Nations Economic Commission for Europe. (1998). *Aarhus Convention.* http://ec.europa.eu/environment/aarhus/legislation.htm

United Nations General Assembly. (2020, July).*Eradicating Rural Poverty to Implement the 2030 Agenda for Sustainable Development.* https://undocs.org/A/75/189

UNDP. (1991). *Human Development Report.* Oxford University Press, Annual.

UNDP. (2022). *Decisions by Topic: Rural Development. Transforming our World: The 2030 Agenda for Sustainable Development.* Retrieved January 1, 2025, from https://sustainabledevelopment.un.org/topics/ruraldevelopment/decisions

United Nations and UNWTO. (2010).*International Recommendations for Tourism Statistics 2008.* United Nations.

Van der Ploeg, J. D., Renting, H., Brunori, G., Knicken, K., Mannion, J., Marsden, T., de Roest, K., Sevilla Guzman, E., & Ventura, F. (2000). Rural Development: From Practices and Policies Towards Theory. *Sociologia Ruralis, 40*(4), 391–408.

William, S. K. T. (1978). *Rural Development in Nigeria Ile Ife.* University of Ife Press.

World Bank. (….). *Rural Population.* Retrieved June 14, 2025, from https://data.worldbank.org/indicator/SP.RUR.TOTL

World Bank. (2004). *World Development Report: Making Services Work for Poor People.* World Bank.

World Bank. (2006). Agricultural Investment Sourcebook. Module 12 "Scaling Up Agricultural Investments in the Bank's Changing Internal Environment". Washington, D.C.

World Bank. (2009a). *Making Development Climate Resilient: A World Bank Strategy for Sub-Saharan Africa.* Report no. 46947-AFR (December). Washington, DC: Sustainable Development Department, World Bank.

World Bank. (2009b). *Transforming Africa's Infrastructure.* Retrieved March 23, 2025, from https://www.worldbank.org/en/news/feature/2009/11/12/transforming-africas-infrastructure

World Bank. (2021a). *Income Generation.* https://www.worldbank.org

World Bank. (2021b). *South Africa Invests in Biodiversity to Promote Rural Development and Conservation.* Retrieved June 17, 2025, from https://www.worldbank.org/en/news/press-release/2021/07/13/south-africa-invests-in-biodiversity-to-promote-rural-development-and-conservation.

World Bank. (2024). *Pathways Out of the Polycrisis: Poverty, Prosperity, and Planet Report.* International Bank for Reconstruction and Development/The World Bank 1818 H Street NW, Washington, DC 20433.

World Bank. (2024). *Pathways Out of the Polycrisis. Poverty, Prosperity, and Planet Report 2024.* International Bank for Reconstruction and Development/The World Bank 1818 H Street NW, Washington, DC 20433.

World Bank (….). *Rural Population (% of Total Population)—Sub-Saharan Africa.* Retrieved June 11, 2025, from https://data.worldbank.org/indicator/SP.RUR.TOTL.ZS?locations=ZG

WHO. (2014). *UN-Water Global Analysis and Assessment of Sanitation and Drinking-Water (GLAAS).* 2014 Report: Investing in Water and Sanitation: Increasing Access, Reducing Inequalities. Geneva. Available from http://www.who.int/iris/handle/10665/139735

Van der Waldt, G. (2014). Infrastructure Project Challenges: The Case of DR Kenneth Kaunda District Municipality. *Journal of Construction Project Management and Innovation, 4*(1), 844–862.

Zavratnik, V., Kos, A., & Duh, E. S. (2018, July). Smart Villages: Comprehensive Review of Initiatives and Practices. *Sustainability, 10*(7), 2559.

Yao, Q. (2019). *Study on Characteristics and Evolutionary Pattern of Architectural Complexity System Based on Architectural Meme Theory* (Ph.D. Thesis). Chongqing University, Chongqing, China.

FSC
www.fsc.org
MIX
Papier | Fördert
gute Waldnutzung
FSC® C083411

Kolibri 360 GmbH
Ferdinand-Jühlke-Straße 7
99095 Erfurt, Deutschland
produktsicherheit@kolibri360.de